GOD SO LOVED

THE BOOKS OF J. SIDLOW BAXTER

AWAKE, MY HEART
Daily devotional meditations for the entire year. These readings are "beautifully simple and simply beautiful, profoundly simple and simply profound." — *Evangelical Christian*

GOING DEEPER
A deeply spiritual study on the theme of knowing, loving and serving our Lord Jesus Christ.

HIS PART AND OURS
Enriching exposition and devotional studies in the reciprocal union of Christ and His people. "A truly great book."
— *Moody Monthly*

GOD SO LOVED
A captivating new presentation of John 3:16. Theological, devotional, practical. In two parts — (1) The New Testament Truth, (2) The Old Testament Type.

STUDIES IN PROBLEM TEXTS
Informing, elucidatory and applicatory expositions of certain Scripture passages which have occasioned perplexity.

MARK THESE MEN
Arresting studies in striking aspects of Bible characters with special relevances for our own times and the days ahead.

EXPLORE THE BOOK
A notable work on the Bible; in one handsome volume of approximately 1800 pages, 6 volumes in one.

GOD SO LOVED

An Expository Series on the Theology and Evangel of the Best-known Text in the Bible

J. SIDLOW BAXTER

ZONDERVAN PUBLISHING HOUSE
Grand Rapids, Michigan

First printing		1960
Second printing		1963
Third printing		1968
Fourth printing	February	1971
Fifth printing	August	1971

PRINTED IN THE UNITED STATES OF AMERICA

I take the liberty of dedicating these chapters to my valued friend and brother in the ministry of the Gospel—

THE REV. R. W. A. MITCHELL,

formerly of England, and now of the United States, with esteem and affection.

FOREWORD TO AMERICAN EDITION

EVER SINCE these chapters were issued in England, some years ago now, under the title, *The Best Word Ever*, they have exercised a rewarding ministry and have been sealed by the Holy Spirit in the true conversion of many persons. Designedly simple, their aim is to explicate and clarify those primal and basal truths of the Gospel which are concentrated in the best-known verse of the Bible, and which, when individually appropriated, save the soul.

Many readers have passed these chapters on to others, whom they were anxious to win for Christ; and we know that in some instances, at least, people have thereby been brought into saving union with our Lord Jesus. The latest grateful victim, so far as I know, was a medical doctor.

These messages were first preached as an evangelistic series. That accounts for their style, which, however, I still opine, helps rather than hinders the average reader. And now the chapters make their debut in an American edition. May a gracious, onlooking Heaven deign still further to use the simple, the imperfect, the unworthy, to the healing or helping of all who chance to read.

J. S. B.

CONTENTS

PART I

THE NEW TESTAMENT TRUTH

PART II

THE OLD TESTAMENT TYPE

NEW TESTAMENT

"For God so loved the world that He gave His only begotten Son, that whosoever believeth in Him should not perish, but have everlasting life."—*John iii.* 16.

OLD TESTAMENT

"And the LORD said unto Moses: Make thee a fiery serpent, and set it upon a pole; and it shall come to pass that every one that is bitten, when he looketh upon it, shall live."—*Numbers xxi.* 8.

"And as Moses lifted up the serpent in the wilderness, even so must the Son of Man be lifted up, that whosoever believeth in Him should not perish, but have eternal life."—*John iii.* 14, 15.

PART ONE

THE NEW TESTAMENT
TRUTH

Like the treacherous signal-boats that are sometimes stationed by wreckers off an iron-bound coast, the shifting systems of false religion are continually changing their places. Like them they attract only to bewilder, and allure only to destroy.

How different from these floating and delusive systems is that unchanging Gospel of Christ which stands forth like the towering lighthouse of Eddystone, with its beacon blaze streaming far out over the midnight sea! The angry waves, through many a long year, have rolled in, thundering against its base. The winds of heaven have warred fiercely around its pinnacle. The rains have dashed against its gleaming lantern. *But there it stands.* It moves not, it trembles not; for it is "founded on a rock." Year after year the storm-stricken mariner looks out for its star-like light as he sweeps in through the English Channel.

So is it with the unchanging Gospel of Christ. While other systems rise and fall, and pass into nothingness, this Gospel (like its immutable Author) is "the same yesterday, to-day, and for ever." While other false and flashing lights are extinguished, this, the "true light," *ever* shineth.

Theodore Cuyler

IS IT REALLY TRUE?

"God so loved the world . . ."—John iii. 16.

"GOD so loved the world . . ." So says the text; but is it really true? Can we still believe it? Europe and America have drifted so far to-day from anything like implicit belief in the teachings of the Bible, that this oft-repeated affirmation of God's love for man seems an "idle tale" to millions of people. There is a widespread breakdown of belief, due to the continued teaching of the Evolution theory in our schools and colleges, and to a pseudo-scholarship which has spent itself in vainly endeavouring to reduce the Bible to the level of a merely human document. Yet deep down, beneath all scepticism and prejudice, there is a wistful yearning in most human hearts for just such an assurance as we have in this great old Gospel truth that "God so loved the world . . ." Many would fain believe it; but their intellectual difficulties seem to block the way like high hurdles.

Perhaps, however, we may take this much for granted even to-day, with most people, that we need not set about arguing for the bare *fact* of God's existence. Even our most unbelieving scientists have not been able to hold out against the evidence for that. Without developing the well-known anthropological, cosmological, historical, ontological, providential, psychological and teleological arguments, we may surely say with all truth that there are ample evidences of God, to any honest mind, even in the outward phenomena of the universe. One of the Red Republicans of 1793 said to a peasant of La Vendée: "We are going to pull down your churches and your steeples,—all that recalls the superstitions of past ages, and all that brings to your mind the idea of God." The peasant replied: "Citizen, pull down the stars then." Lord Bacon said that he would think it more rational to believe all the fables in all the poets, the legends, the Talmud, and the Koran, than to believe that this vast and wonderful universe could exist without a Creator and Controller.

The universe could not have come into being without a Creator, for out of nothing nothing comes. Scientific discovery has settled with absolute finality that this universe can neither be eternal nor self-evolved. This universe implies creation: and creation implies a Creator. The marvellous order and regularity which are everywhere observable throughout the universe, which enable men of science to foretell an eclipse centuries before its occurrence, and our gardeners to say that a daffodil will come from one bulb and a hyacinth from another, not to mention an endless variety of other instances, point to a causal Mind; for out of chaos only chaos evolves; and order implies a Mind. We talk about the "laws" of nature; but as John Stuart Mill said, "The laws of nature cannot account for their own origin." The presence of laws implies a Lawgiver.

Writing in *The American Magazine* not long ago, a manufacturer expressed himself thus: "It takes a girl in our factory about two days to learn to put the seventeen parts of a meat chopper together. It may be that these millions of worlds, all balanced so wonderfully in space—it may be that they just happened; it may be by a billion years of tumbling about they finally arranged themselves. I don't know. I am merely a plain manufacturer of cutlery. But this I do know: that you can shake the seventeen parts of a meat chopper around in a wash-tub for the next seventeen billion years, and you'll never make a meat chopper."

But we need say no more along this line; for as the footprint in the sand is sufficient to attest the presence of a man, so, to common sense and common honesty, the impress of God, which we see everywhere around us, is sufficient to attest the reality of the Divine presence and power in the universe. Moreover, I think it is true to say that most of those people who have difficulty in believing that God loves this world are people who would be far from calling themselves atheists. They readily assent to the fact that God is; but they cannot believe that God really loves this world, and that for various reasons.

THE DISCOVERIES OF SCIENCE

There are those, for instance, who find it incompatible with scientific discovery. They would say that it is impossible to believe it in view of *the insignificance of our world*. In a former day, when this little planet on which we live was thought to be the biggest thing that God had made, and the centre of the universe, it was easy to believe in John iii. 16, with its message of "God so loved the world." But the discoveries of our astronomers have shaken men's ideas up a good deal during the last few generations. Far from this earth's being the centre of the universe, it is now seen to be an almost infinitesimal speck amid a bewilderingly exhaustless profusion of suns and systems and constellations and nebulae which staggers the mind. Beyond our own little solar system, countless other suns and systems far more illustrious than ours stretch away in vast variety—blazing super-stars beyond estimation, around which swing myriads of globes with their belts and rings and treasures, immeasurable thoroughfares of glory, ocean after ocean of constellations, colossal stars which could absorb our own sun and planets without adding one beam to their splendour or a sprinkling of dust to their magnitude—burning stars which are only kept from destroying us because of the immense expanses intervening—groups of stars like gigantic stellar cities, choirs of worlds, and crowded congregations of celestial marvels—and still no sign of the universe's border, or of the hem on creation's garment of space!

What a single leaf is to the mighty forests of the Amazon, what a single blade of grass is to the American prairies and the Russian steppes, what a single drop of dew is to a thousand Pacifics, such is the big, little orb on which we live! And if the revolving ball on which man lives is so humiliatingly outclassed, what is man himself? Does it not need a microscopic eye to see him at all? Over against the universe's immensity is man's infinitesimalness. Over against the universe's solidarity is man's fragility. Over against the universe's continuingness is man's fleetingness. Estimated on the basis of comparative dimension, we may ask almost despairingly nowadays, "What is man?"

THE THEOLOGICAL PROBLEM

In view of all this, can it be said that God even notices this world, let alone values it so pre-eminently as to make it the object of the supreme expression of His love? If the creation is so great, how much greater must be the Creator! If the edifice is so vast and magnificent, how incomprehensibly tremendous must be the Architect! And if God be such, and this tiny world be such, is it not a bit of pathetic credulity to say any longer that God *loves* it?

When the old-fashioned Ptolemaic conception of the universe began breaking to pieces, about the time of the Reformation— as the earth shrivelled into comparative insignificance, and the universe around it increased into awesome magnitude, theologians and ecclesiastical leaders began to turn pale. It seemed as though the very foundation of Christianity was becoming jeopardised. Now that the earth was diminishing to an almost trivial entity in a teeming realm of bodies, how could it any longer be proclaimed that "God so loved the world that He gave His only begotten Son, that whosoever believeth in Him should not perish, but have everlasting life"? Accordingly, men like the famous Polish astronomer, Nicolaus Copernicus, and Galileo Galilei, who was the first to apply the telescope to the study of the heavens, had a bad time of it. The latter was made to abjure the new "science" under the torture of the Roman Catholic "Inquisition"! But it was no use—the dark night of the mediaeval ages was compelled to slink away before the dawning of the new era of Science: and we now know, as men never knew before, the colossal dimensions of the universe.

Well, what then? Can we still say with as much truth and meaning as before, that God loves this little world? We can. Indeed we can say it with even more fulness of meaning and glory; for science has proved in this, as in other ways, the hand-maid of Christian theology. When the troublesome new discoveries began to disturb Christian faith overmuch, it occurred to one rather thoughtful theologian to remind folks that after all there is no such thing as "big" or "little" with a God Who is *infinite*. God does not love this world for its physical size,

but for its *moral value*! All that the new discoveries were really
doing was to give us a bigger and more glorious God, and a
profounder conception of the wonder of that Divine love which
expressed itself through the historical facts on which Christianity
is built.

THE VITAL FACT

Ah yes, that is the fact to grasp—God does not love this
world for its physical size, but for its *moral value*. After all,
what is matter compared with mind? What is a star compared
with a soul? What is an inanimate constellation compared with
a God-conscious intellect? In my book, *His Part and Ours*, I
have mentioned an incident which forcibly illustrates the point
we are making just here. A leading British scientist wrote in
one of our well-known newspapers concerning the vastness of the
universe as known to modern astronomy, and somewhat des-
pisingly asked—"Astronomically speaking, what is *man*?" A
reader replied, begging to inform him that "astronomically
speaking" man is the *astronomer*! Well did the Lord Jesus know
the value of one immortal human soul when He asked: "What
shall it profit a man if he gain the whole world, and lose his own
soul?" Men can measure worlds swung out in space; but who
can measure the breadths and lengths and depths and heights
of one human soul? And who then shall even faintly sense the
unutterable value of the whole human race? And who now,
with materialistically-minded stupidity, will put the bigness of
mere matter against the intellectuality, spirituality, and immortality of man? The biggest of the stars is blind. It can be seen
but cannot see. It can be weighed and measured and analysed;
but it cannot know or feel. It may be admired; but it cannot
love. What means the biggest star to an omnipotent God when
compared with a soul made in the very image of God Himself
—a soul with the capacity for God, for holiness and fellowship
and worship and service and adoration and love?—and with
equally real capabilities of sin and shame and agony of suffering? Ah, John iii. 16 is in no danger from the discoveries of the
telescope. If only man could invent a telescope to look into the
spiritual realm he would never again ask: "Astronomically

speaking, what is man?" As the physical universe grows bigger
and still bigger to the eye of the telescope, all that happens is
that our conception of the Divine majesty deepens more and
more, so that instead of fearing that scientific discovery jeopardises
John iii. 16, we find ourselves—even more than our fathers—
lost in wonder, love, and praise, that "God so loved the world
that He gave His only begotten Son, that whosoever believeth
in Him should not perish, but have everlasting life."

OTHER OBJECTIONS

Of course, there are other supposed reasons for rejecting the
Gospel message of God's love for this world, besides that which
we have mentioned, though that is perhaps the most common
among people who believe in the fact of God at all.

For instance, there is the old idea of Deism, that the *transcendence* of God excludes any thought of His being interested in the
affairs of this world. The Supreme is too exalted to concern
Himself with such a trifle. He made the world, conditioned it by
certain laws, endowed matter with its properties, and rational
beings with the powers of free agency, and then left the world
to the guidance of these general laws. Therefore He now has no
immediate interest in the things of this earth. He deals with it
only distantly and mediately through the operation of the laws
which He has super-imposed for its orderly running.

The answer to this is clear. Over against the assertion that
God is too transcendent to condescend to any interest in this
world is the fact that *He condescended to create it*. Yea, more—
if God does not love this world, then why did He create it at
all? And still more, as Science is ever more clearly demon-
strating, God is not only transcendent above His creation, but
is everywhere *immanent* within it, "giving life and breath" to
all, as the vital environment in which we "live and move and
have our being."

Then there are those who say they cannot believe in the love
of God for us because of His *seeming unreality*. But how can
people expect God to be real to them when they cannot spare
more than five minutes a day, even if they spare that much time,

for prayer to Him, or to contemplate Him gratefully? The cold unresponsiveness of such hearts is sufficient in itself to ensure the unreality of God! Either God is pushed to the back, or is pushed completely out of thought, and then the complaint is made that God seems unreal! He will be real enough to such in a day yet to be!

But need we mention other objections to this precious truth of God's love for man? Nay, one would think that poor, sinful human hearts would be only too eager to seize such news and embrace such a Gospel! To those who feel sincere doubts about the love of God, we would pass on the word of the old Puritan theologian—*never let what you DON'T know disturb your faith in what you DO know.* As we look out upon this vast and wonderful universe, and as we face the present problem of human sin and suffering, we must admit that there are many things which seem mysterious. Again and again we simply have to say that we just *do not know.* But let us weigh this well—that however much there is that we do not yet know, it does not and cannot destroy the truth of that which we really do know—that which really *is.* The old Puritan is right.

Our ignorance about many things does not in the slightest degree affect those solid historical facts upon which Christianity is built. It is a fact that God is, and that He has revealed Himself in the Person of the Lord Jesus Christ. It is a solid, glorious fact of history, that Jesus came, that He lived, taught, wrought, suffered, died, rose, and ascended to the Father again. Yes, He rose, and He lives to-day—the everliving, everloving, everlasting Saviour of all who receive Him; and the dear old text still shines with the unquenched and unquenchable light of eternal truth— "For God so loved the world that He gave His only begotten Son, that whosoever believeth in Him should not perish, but have everlasting life."

Yes, the great truth is there before us, written in the book that never lies, and coming to us from the lips of the incarnate Son of God Himself—if, as seems, it was Jesus who said the words, not John the narrator. And, since the words were first spoken to a solitary seeker after truth, shall not we ourselves also receive them to our hearts as individual sinners, needing

to be saved from the guilt and power of our sin? See that lovely
word "Whosoever." It looks out to all four points of the compass.
It throws its arms round all five continents. It bids us come
from North and South and East and West, and find salvation
in the atonement made by God's dear Son. It beckons to young
and old, to high and low, to rich and poor, and overleaps all
distinctions of race and caste and colour in its gracious eagerness
to draw us back to the forgiving Father who loves us, and gave
His Son to save us. Read the words again. They are for *you*.
Take them to your own heart. By a simple act of faith accept
the Saviour now, and become saved.

After the freeing of the American slaves, the freed men exhibited a keen desire to learn reading and writing. One old
uncle greatly wanted to learn to read so that he might read the
Bible, but cared nothing about learning how to write. His one
thought was to read for himself the words of God's book. As
soon as he was able to spell out the words, he studied out the
verse: "God so loved the world that He gave His only begotten
Son, that whosoever believeth in Him should not perish, but
have everlasting life." By the time he had got to the middle
of the verse his feelings had overcome him, and with a broken
voice he asked: "Is dis ra'al? Is dis de surenuff word ob de Lord?"
His teacher assured him that there was no doubt about it. It
was really the Lord's own word. And the old uncle exclaimed
softly: "Tink ob it—uncle readin' it for hisself!" When he had
finished reading the verse, he said: "Now, if old uncle dies, he
kin go up dar, and tell de good Lord Jesus dat he read it in His
own book—'Whomsumever b'liebes on Him shan't perish, but
hab eberlasting life'; and de Lord knows dat Uncle Sam b'liebes
on'm, 'cause he read it for hisself in His own book."

There is something touching in the quaintness as well as in
the simplicity of the old uncle's childlike trust. The one vital
question to his mind—and it is the vital question in every serious,
seeking mind—was: Is this the "surenuff" word of God? The
answer is: Yes; this is indeed the word of the living, loving
God to us men and women. And what a word it is! What love
it expresses! What a Saviour it offers! What an opportunity
it presents! Let us gladly receive it. Let us make haste to the

Saviour. We need have no fear. We need not delay. It is indeed the word of God; and it says "whosoever."

Jesus the Saviour, this Gospel to tell,
    Joyfully came;
Came with the helpless and hopeless to dwell,
    Sharing their sorrow and shame;
Seeking the lost, seeking the lost,
Saving, redeeming, at measureless cost.

Jesus is seeking the wanderers yet.
    Why do they roam?
Love only waits to forgive and forget.
    Home! weary wanderers, home!
Wonderful love, wonderful love,
Dwells in the heart of the Father above.

WHAT ABOUT PAIN?

O Joy that seekest me through pain,
  I cannot close my heart to Thee;
I trace the rainbow through the rain,
And feel the promise is not vain,
  That morn shall tearless be.

George Matheson

I dimly guess from blessings known
  Of greater out of sight,
And with the chastened psalmist own
  His judgments too are right.

J. G. Whittier

Judge not the Lord by feeble sense,
  But trust Him for His grace;
Behind a frowning providence
  He hides a smiling face.

William Cowper

WHAT ABOUT PAIN?

"God so loved the world"—John iii. 16.

FOLLOWING up our last address, perhaps we ought now to give special thought to another class of people who profess inability to believe that God loves this world. These tell us that they cannot believe it because of its *irreconcilableness with the prevalence of suffering upon earth.*

"Look at the *physical* suffering which blights the race," they exclaim—"the untold physical suffering inflicted by sickness and disease and accident and the forces of nature over which man has no control. Look at the *mental* suffering which flogs men as by a scourge of curses—the mental suffering inflicted by social inequalities and injustices, by poverty and adversity, by hatreds and strife, by moral evil and by death, and by that monstrous outrage, war! How can all this be reconciled with the supposed love of God for this world?"

Well, we are quick to appreciate the poignancy of this problem, for we ourselves have suffered and have sympathetically shared in the sufferings of others. Moreover, we are far from daring to claim that we can clear up this mystery of suffering; nor are we unaware that all merely human philosophies break down pathetically in their struggle after some satisfying solution. Yet, for all that, we will not hesitate to say that there is far more light on this problem than most people realise—light which, in our own judgment, makes it intelligently compatible with the Gospel message that "God so loved the world . . ."

THE BIBLICAL REVELATION

First, we should view this problem *in the full sweep of Biblical revelation.* Few people sense what enlightenment we owe to the

Bible. Few people have any idea what ignorance and chaos we should now have been in without it. Few people have any intelligent acquaintance with what the Bible teaches about the place of suffering in human history. The Bible teaches that this world, in its present condition, is neither as God originally created it nor as He ultimately purposes it. We shall not take time here arguing against the evolutionary or spontaneous generation theory of man's origin; for, as is now well known, that theory is utterly unproven.

The Bible recognises a difference between what we may call God's *directive* will and His *permissive* will. We may mentally picture these as being two straight horizontal lines, the one below the other—the higher one being the line of God's *directive* will, and the lower one being the line of His *permissive* will. Now when God reconstituted this earth to become the habitation of man, as described in Genesis, this world—the system of things as then originated on the earth—was in the line of God's directive will; that is, it was in the line of His ultimate purpose for mankind, and was according to His direct intent. Man was created in a condition of sinlessness, and was called to fellowship with God in the fulfilling of high and holy purpose. But man, being made "in the image of God," was endowed with that God-like attribute, free-will; and through man's disobedient exercise of that power, sin entered into the human race, alienating man from God. Thus, with the incoming of sin, this world fell to the lower level of God's *intermediate* or "permissive" will.

In the foreknowledge of God this was anticipated and provided for. God's answer to it was the provision of THE SAVIOUR, THE LORD JESUS CHRIST, SON OF GOD AND SAVIOUR OF MEN, who should come in "the fulness of time" to redeem the race (as recorded in the New Testament), and in whom the world should eventually be lifted back on to the line of God's directive will and ultimate purpose (as shown in I Corinthians xv and the last two chapters of the New Testament)—toward which consummation the closing decades of this present age are rapidly running up.

Man, being possessed of intellect, moral consciousness, and free-will, obviously cannot be *coerced* into virtue. God has created human spirits with a constitution which involves free agency and a power—within necessary limits—to do their own will even though it be opposed to His own. Arbitrary enforcement of His will upon such would be a violation of their nature. Clearly, the will of God that men should be virtuous cannot be enforced upon men, for any action that is enforced is not virtuous. Therefore, during the present intermediate period, sin and suffering are permitted, but are overruled to the spiritual education and highest good of men. In the end it will be seen that accident and sickness and all other sufferings have been overruled to a beneficent end, though at present they seem tragic and costly. What an accumulated mass of evidence there is already, gathered from the experience of millions, to prove that suffering has been blessed of God to bring souls into a saving knowledge of Himself! What tuition is imparted, what sympathy inwrought, what insight given, what character developed, in suffering! Not that suffering itself is blessed; but it is beneficently overruled in anticipation of the coming consummation when the world shall be lifted back to the higher level of God's first and final purpose. Then shall all tears be wiped away.

God has never abandoned His Edenic ideal for man; and although in the end the Garden has given place to the City, and the one man has become a race, yet the original ideal shall be realised, and the intended goal be reached. It is to help our poor minds to bear the seeming enigmas of human experience that the Bible reveals enough of man's earliest past and enough of his ultimate future to enable us to grasp at least something of the sweep and meaning of the ages. "The whole creation groaneth and travaileth in pain together until now," says Paul (Rom. viii. 22); but he also says: "The creation itself shall be delivered from the bondage of corruption."

This present intermediate period of God's permissive will, then, other than being incompatible with God's love, is really the expression of His loving *patience* with sinful man, as He brings him through permitted, but self-inflicted suffering, to the final triumph of the right and good. So teaches the Bible. Not all is revealed. Big mysteries remain. But this explanation of the past and this guarantee concerning the ultimate give a flood of light.

THE DIVINE RELATIONSHIP

Then again, the problem of suffering must be seen *in the full sweep of God's relationship with the world*. Generally speaking, *a priori* reasoning is not so forcible as the inductive, or *a posteriori* method; yet we are certainly safe in arguing from the following propositions—(1) God is the *source* of the universe; (2) God is a free Spirit, *greater* than the universe; (3) God has a uniform *method* in conducting the universe; (4) God has a *purpose* in the universe. The order, unity, uniformity, and method which pervade the universe attest the presence of such a purpose.

Yes, God must have a purpose in the universe; and it follows that this purpose must be a *good* purpose. It is impossible to think of a *bad* Creator; for if the source of all be evil, where does good come from? and where does the innate human recognition of, and desire for, the good come from?—not to mention the countless evidences of a good purpose all around us in the realm of nature. Beyond doubt there is a good purpose in the universe; and the problem of present pain does not annul this any more than problems which lie in the line of scientific research annul the well-established general findings of Science.

The problem of pain arises out of the constitution of man. We have touched on this already. Obviously, God could only create beings capable of goodness, holiness, love, and fellowship with Himself, by constituting them free agents. An automaton has no moral sense or value. God has therefore willed other wills into existence, each having a limited but genuine field of sovereignty. It is clear that such creation of free beings involves the possibility of results which the will of God would not have produced had it kept the field to itself. But there could be no creating of beings in the image of God Himself without this contingency. Coming down to the realm of actual fact, God created man "in His own image." Man sinned—and fell. Man still sins—and suffers.

But what now about God's government of the world? How does it relate to the sin of free beings? Well, to fall back on another *a priori* necessity, the omniscient God must have foreknown the sin of His creatures, and have predetermined its subserviency to the further reach of His purpose. But it may be asked how even God Himself can ensure the final outcome if He has called such free beings into existence. Surely the acts of free beings cannot be predestined, for predestined acts are not those of free beings; and how, then, in a dealing with free agents, can the final outcome be predetermined?

The answer is—as we have said elsewhere—that God, in His government of this world, leaves enough scope for the free action of the human will to make men conscious at all times that they are acting of themselves and by their own intelligent choice; but He does not allow His larger purposes for the human race to rest upon the uncertain behaviour of the human will. God foreknows all things; and arising from His foreknowledge is His sovereign predetermining of ultimate issues, and His over-ruling of all intermediate developments, however seemingly contrary, to the predetermined end.

This may be illustrated by reference to the unbelief of the Jewish nation when Christ came, according to Old Testament prophecy, and offered Himself as Messiah-King of Israel. Did this unbelief thwart God's larger purpose? No; it was foreknown and overruled. In sovereign super-control God caused even the crucifixion of Israel's Messiah to become the coronation of the world's Saviour. Instead of God's purpose having become frustrated, there emerges from the very ruins of Jewish unbelief God's further movement through the Christian Church, and the proclaiming of a world-embracing Gospel of salvation to the Gentiles.

Moreover, God has the power, mysterious as it seems to us, of guiding free beings from above their freedom, and without interfering with it. Dr. W. N. Clarke says: "The manner of this higher control is above our observation; yet there is something analogous to it in the relations of men. The most effective controlling influence that is exercised by men among themselves is not exercised through dictation or constraint; it is the work of superior mind, exerted upon men in their freedom. The higher judgment, wisdom, efficiency, and personal force of one can influence the action of another, without suppressing any worthy quality in that other. One secures from another the doing of some noble thing that he desires, while the other's will, far from being crushed, is acting at its noblest. Some men show ability to rule conflicting forces and bring into their service wills that are at cross-purposes with them and with one another. We often say that the business of a great establishment is the work of a single mind, directing, co-ordinating, and turning to the best use the energies of a hundred minds, or of a thousand, which do their best work under this strong and intelligent organising influence. All such acts of personal power on the part of men are indeed imperfect, but they help us to imagine a higher control on the part of God, preserving human freedom, and yet using free men for higher purposes than their own."

Yes, without violating the freedom of the human will, God, as the good Creator, exercises full control throughout the universe, thereby guaranteeing the final fruition of His all-comprehending purpose; and in the compassing of this grand purpose even the sin and suffering of the present phase are accommodated and made to contribute.

Yes, even the permission of *war* can be reconciled with this far-reaching purpose of good. Even as I now speak, a war rages, and people are still asking: "Why does God permit war?" Yet, as we have seen, within limits God accords the human will a real freedom—enough freedom, certainly, for it to be quite clear that war—the present war—is man's own doing, brought on himself by his own wrong-doing, hatred, and godless folly; and if man stubbornly refuses to learn the folly and tragedy of godlessness except by bringing upon himself the blood and agony of war, then he shall be permitted to learn in that way. Let us say it boldly—we believe, in the light of Biblical revelation, that in the final issue of things it will be seen that even war has been a sadly necessary permission in the education of our fallen race.

No; we are not excusing war, or the sin which causes war. We deplore it. We denounce it. But ponder this—Suppose God had marshalled the whole human race before Him in the early phases of human history and proclaimed to them the folly and tragedy of sin and war; do you think that the race would have learned the lesson? History is a sufficient commentary on the heart of man to convince us otherwise. Man knows the right and does the wrong. If, then, man refuses to learn by any other way, he shall learn at long last, through the very blood and agony which he is permitted to bring upon himself, that he simply cannot get on without God. In the end man *shall* indeed have learned, in the school of self-inflicted suffering, that he needs the King of God's own appointing, even the Lord Jesus Christ. Perhaps the time when our race will have learned this lesson is nearer than many of us are thinking.

THE TESTIMONY OF HISTORY

But there is one more word we would add, namely—we must view this problem of suffering *in the full sweep of history*. Admittedly, if we look merely at disconnected strips of history, or at different communities in isolation, it is often easy to see a muddle rather than a meaning, perversion rather than purpose, and the conflicting ambitions of human greed rather than an all-shaping guidance of God. But if we take history as a whole, watching the movement of the centuries, we see the purpose of the Almighty marching down the ages with irresistible tread, and pushing on to that "one far-off Divine event to which the whole creation moves."

Thoughtful minds have always been impressed by the sense that a firm and steady power, mightier than man, controls the transpirings of time. But we are not left merely in the realm of surmise, for there is one tremendous bit of history which shows us beyond any peradventure that we may reconcile present suffering with the fact of God's love for this world. It is the history of Jesus Christ as given by the four historians of the New Testament. Here we are treading on scientifically tested and proven ground. We are dealing, not with mere theory or philosophy, but with authentic history.

Dr. R. A. Torrey says: "Men of the most remarkable genius, of the profoundest scholarship, of untiring activity, have struggled to pull to pieces the history of Jesus Christ as recorded in the four gospels, and every effort of that kind has met with utter failure. The strongest, the ablest, the most remarkable and

scholarly effort ever made was that of David Strauss, in the
Leben Jesu. It seemed to some for a while as if David Strauss
had succeeded in taking out of the life of Jesus of Nazareth
many things commonly believed. But when the life of Jesus
Christ by the great German rationalist was itself subjected to
criticism, it went to pieces, until there was nothing left. It was
utterly discredited. It would not bear careful and candid examination. Renan, with rare subtlety and literary deftness, endea-
voured to succeed where Strauss had failed. But his own attempt
to eliminate the supernatural from the life of Jesus was less able
in almost every way than that of his German predecessor, and
failed completely. And every other similar effort to pull to pieces
and discredit the life of Jesus Christ, as recorded in the four
gospels, has failed absolutely. And to-day it stands established
beyond the possibility of candid question that Jesus lived and
acted at least substantially—I believe far more than that—as
recorded in the four gospels. It is absolutely impossible for a
man to sit down before the four gospels with an unbiased and
honest mind, determined to find out the truth, and come to any
other conclusion than that this four-gospel record of the life
and words and works of Jesus is substantially accurate history."

Now, as Dr. Torrey continues, if Jesus lived as the New Testament record declares, if He wrought, as the record says He
wrought—healed the sick, cleansed the leper, raised the dead,
and wrought the other miraculous works attributed to Him,
and if, above all, having been put to death, He was raised from
the dead, it proves beyond all question that back of the works
He performed, back of the resurrection of Jesus Christ, is
GOD.

Yes, in the person of the Lord Jesus Christ, the Eternal Himself has entered into our human life, has assumed our nature,
lived our life, shared our lot, felt our woes, and—sublimest of all
mysteries—has borne the guilt and penalty of our sins, expiating
them in the substitutionary suffering of Calvary, satisfying the
claims of His own holy law against us poor sinners, and providing
eternal salvation for all who will by faith appropriate it. Oh,
see the incarnate God nailed to that awful, wondrous, glorious
Cross! "God was in Christ reconciling the world unto Himself."

He weeps, groans, bleeds, and dies that bitterest of all deaths
due to sin. Oh, that marvel of love! The Creator becomes the
Redeemer!

> Could we with ink the ocean fill,
>   And were the sky of parchment made,
> Were every blade of grass a quill,
>   And every man a scribe by trade,—
> To write the love of God above
>   Would drain the ocean dry,
> Nor could the scroll contain the whole,
>   Though writ from sky to sky.

Even now we are far from fully grasping the meaning of permitted suffering; but the whole problem becomes sublimated in
the light of this amazing fact that the Eternal Himself has suffered
with us and *for* us in the redeeming miracle of the Cross.

Yes, despite the suffering and sorrow which sin has poured
into man's cup, it is still true that God loves this world. The
groans and cries of earth's sin-caused travail do not drown the
comforting accents of the Evangel—"For God so loved the world
that He gave His only begotten Son, that whosoever believeth
in Him should not perish, but have everlasting life."

THE TEXT OF TEXTS

O how unlike the complex works of man,
Heaven's easy, artless, unencumbered plan!
No meretricious graces to beguile,
No clustering ornaments to clog the pile;
From ostentation as from weakness free,
It stands like the cerulean arch we see,
Majestic in its own simplicity.
Inscrib'd above the portal, from afar
Conspicuous, as the brightness of a star;
Legible only by the light they give,
Stand the soul-quick'ning words—Believe
    and Live!

William Cowper

THE TEXT OF TEXTS

"For God so loved the world that He gave His only begotten Son, that whosoever believeth in Him should not perish, but have everlasting life."—John iii. 16.

THIS is the best-known text in the Bible. Dr. Carnegie Simpson has called it "The superb commonplace of Christianity." A thousand pities that long familiarity with the words blinds many a mind to their infinite sublimity and boundless wonder!

BY WAY OF COMPARISON

What a wonderful place is London! When, as a young Lancashire laddie, I used to go with my mother to Manchester, and see the big buildings and thronged thoroughfares of that busy "Cotton Metropolis," I thought that no place could ever be greater than Manchester. But the mental boundaries of my boyhood days quickly gave way to wider horizons when later I made contact with London; for after all—and with all respect to my fellow Lancastrians—what is a Manchester to a London?—London, the metropolis of Britain, and the hub of the British Empire. All the great railways lead to London. All the great roadways lead to London. All the main Empire sea-routes seem directly or indirectly connected to London.

Now what London has been for so long to Britain and to the British Empire, this glorious text, John iii. 16, is to the Scriptures. It is the metropolis of Gospel truth. It is the hub of the Bible. It is the vital centre of Divine revelation, and the very heart of the Evangel. All the great truths of the Old Testament converge toward it. All the great doctrines of the New Testament emerge from it. The high-roads of ancient history make for it. The deep sea-routes of profound prophecies lead to it. The redeeming

35

realities of the New Covenant in Jesus' blood are all enfolded in it and unfolded from it.

To make another comparison—what the *sun* is to our solar system, John iii. 16 is in its relation to the Christian message. As Mercury and Venus and the Earth and Mars and the minor planets and Jupiter and Saturn and Uranus and far-away Neptune range in their ceaseless rotation round the central magnet of fire, and receive their illumination from it, so all the distinctive truths of redemption—the riches of the Divine grace, the forgiveness of sins, propitiation, reconciliation, justification, eternal salvation and glorification—revolve round this supreme statement of God's redeeming love, like lamps of silver in fallen man's dark sky.

Once again; what the broadcasting station is to the radio world, John iii. 16 is to human history. Heaven's superlative message to men has thrilled out on the airwaves of time—God *loves!* God *gives!* God *saves!* Oh that a world of sinners might "listen in"! Well may we say, in the words of the old Book, "He that hath ears to hear, let him hear"!

BY WAY OF EXAMINATION

Let us now look carefully at the verse itself, and see it broken up into its constituent parts as light is broken into its contributory colours by the prism. To begin with, we observe that this verse is built around ten great words which stand out in the bigness of their meaning—

1. God	6. Whosoever
2. Loved	7. Believeth
3. World	8. Perish
4. Gave	9. Have
5. Son	10. Life

These ten words, grouped together in this one verse, constitute a significant union of terms. They are ten of the greatest words in the Bible. Indeed, it would not be far from the mark to say that in an outstanding sense they are the ten *distinctive* words of Divine revelation. The message of the whole written word of God is comprehended in them as in no others.

One of the most amazing phenomena of the Bible is its marvellous unity amid diversity. Is there in any other known book a wider diversity going with a more strongly marked unity than we have in the Bible? Centuries elapsed in the writing of it. Over forty different writers contributed to it. These forty odd contributors were persons living at different times and in different places, having differing stations in life, and differing vocabularies and widely differing idiosyncrasies. They wrote to different persons, about different subjects, and for different purposes, not to mention many further variations. Yet the inspiring Spirit of God, who was behind each writer, has so overruled, that despite all the variety and diversity, certain great words and truths run through the entire sixty-six-books-in-one, like the links of a shining chain.

Now the remarkable thing seems to be that all these big, distinctive words are picked out, and packed into this one peerless verse, John iii. 16, as though the Spirit of God had been at pains to gather up into focal expression the supreme truths of the Bible and the Gospel.

But besides this, when we look a little more closely at these ten words, we find, as the late Dr. A. T. Pierson pointed out, that they go together in five deeply significant pairs.

The first pair—the two words "*God*" and "*Son*"—show us the supreme Giver and the supreme Gift, God the Father and Christ the Saviour, two of the ever-blessed Trinity of the Godhead, co-operating in the effecting of our salvation. The second pair show us the two expressions of the Divine benevolence—God "*loved*" and God "*gave*." The third pair show us the two-fold direction of God's loving and giving—the "*world*" and "*whosoever*." The fourth pair show us the two things that all human beings are privileged and invited to do, namely—"*believe*" and "*have*." The fifth pair show us the two ultimate extremes of human destiny—in the one case "*perish*," in the other "*life*." Truly these are five deeply significant pairs of words!

But we may go even further; for it will be observed that in each of these pairs the second term grows out of the first. This is obvious in the case of the first pair—the two words, "God"

and "Son." That word "God" is the comprehensive name for
the Deity; but now, emerging from the mystery of the Divine
being, and coming to us through the miracle of the Incarnation,
is One who, while being "very God of very God" bears the
name of the "Son."

Take the second pair of words—"loved" and "gave." The
giving grows out of the loving. Had God not loved He would
not have given. God does not love us *because* Jesus died for us
—as some have mistakenly supposed. No; it is the other way
round—the Son of God died to redeem us because God already
loved us. Despite the plain teaching of the New Testament,
many people have held the erroneous idea that God the First
Person is a kind of hard, cold, revengeful Judge who looks down
upon this world of human sinners with nothing but an unsym-
pathetic determination to judge and punish—and that the tender-
hearted Lord Jesus, in pity for us, came between this wrathful
Judge and ourselves, and died for us, so that at any rate the
offended Judge might try to feel *some* merciful relentings towards
us.

D. L. Moody, the famous evangelist, tells us that this was the
idea which filled his own mind in the earlier years. Later, he
came to see that this was a tragic caricature of the real Gospel.
It certainly *is* a tragic caricature. Let us banish it from our minds
forever. Christ's redemptive work for us is the *proof* of the
Father's love, not the *cause* of it. Yes, note the order—He
"loved" and then "gave."

See, now, the third pair of words—the "world" and "whosoever." Once again the second grows out of the first. The "world"
—that is *all* of us. "Whosoever"—that is *each* of us. The one
term is collective: the other is individualistic. It is good to know
that God loves us *all*, without exception or distinction. It is
better still to know that besides this, God singles out each one
of us, and makes each of us the special object of His loving
concern.

And now see the fourth pair of words—"believeth" and "have."
How clearly again the second grows out of the first! It is by
believing that we *have*. How graciously simple God has made

the way of salvation! Yet how stupidly slow many of us are to grasp it! Lots of people think that if only they might first *have*, then they could *believe*. They want to have all their intellectual difficulties solved, for instance, before they can "believe." If only such people would take God at His word, and believe upon the Saviour for the salvation of their souls, they would come to know by experience that believing is having. One ounce of real experience is worth more than tons of hypothetical objections, even as one glorious diamond is worth more than tons of common house coal.

Finally, the same is true of the fifth pair—"perish" and "life." That word "perish" covers all outside Christ, for there is no eternal life outside Christ. A perishing world! Nay, there is another word to add; for emerging from the ranks of the human race there come forth a mighty host who have found salvation and eternal life in Jesus Christ. How vast that mighty host only that great day to come will declare; but from the word of God we *do* know already that it is "a great multitude which no man could number, of all nations and kindreds and people and tongues," standing "before the throne, and before the Lamb, clothed with white robes (symbol of purity) and having palms (symbol of victory) in their hands." The important concern for ourselves here and now, is to make quite sure that individually we have made the Lord Jesus our own Saviour.

Thus in John iii. 16, we have the ten distinctive words of Scripture, going in five significant pairs, with the second term in each pair growing out of the first. Truly, in this verse of verses we have the whole Bible in miniature, and the quintessence of the Gospel. Oh, let the eye linger gratefully over the immortal words again:

"FOR GOD SO LOVED THE WORLD THAT HE GAVE HIS ONLY BEGOTTEN SON, THAT WHOSOEVER BELIEVETH IN HIM SHOULD NOT PERISH, BUT HAVE EVERLASTING LIFE."

Such then is our text of texts briefly reviewed by way of simple outward comparison and inward examination.

BY WAY OF PARALLEL

And now look at this verse in the light of another great text in the New Testament. There is a parallel too plain to be missed between John iii. 16 and Ephesians iii. 18. In this Ephesian verse, Paul speaks of "the breadth and length and depth and height" of the love of Christ. His prayer to God for us is, "That He (God) would grant you, according to the riches of His glory, to be strengthened with might by His Spirit in the inner man; that Christ may dwell in your hearts by faith; that ye, being rooted and grounded in love, may be able to comprehend with all the saints what is the *BREADTH* and *LENGTH* and *DEPTH* and *HEIGHT*, and to know the love of Christ which passeth knowledge." (Eph. iii. 16–19.)

Look, then, at John iii. 16 in the light of Ephesians iii. 18, and see the breadth and length and depth and height of God's glorious love. "God so loved the *world*"—there is the *BREADTH*. "That He *gave His only begotten Son*"—there is the *LENGTH* to which His love would go. "That whosoever believeth in Him should not *perish*"—there is the ghastly *DEPTH* from which His love comes to save us. "But have *everlasting life*"—there is the wondrous *HEIGHT* to which His love can lift us.

"Breadth and length and depth and height"—does it seem strange that Paul should speak of the love of Christ as having these four dimensions? Breadth and length and depth and height, strictly speaking, are characteristics which can only be predicated of material objects; they do not appertain to abstract concepts such as love, joy, hope, peace, fear, or to any purely mental notion. Perhaps if we had not grown so accustomed to Paul's phraseology here we would be more readily struck by its peculiarity.

What is it that Paul has in mind in so speaking? I think the Bible itself can best interpret that for us. Away back in earlier Old Testament times, when God instructed Moses to make that marvellously symbolical and typical structure, the Tabernacle, He told Moses to make first of all the Holy of Holies, the inmost shrine, where Jehovah Himself should reveal His presence among His people. The Holy of Holies must be ten cubits long and ten cubits wide by ten cubits high. In other words, its breadth and length and depth or height were all to be equal with each other, that is, ten by ten by ten cubits. In later years, when Solomon built the magnificent Jerusalem temple which superseded the Tabernacle, he made the length of the Holy of Holies *twenty* cubits; but he also made the breadth and height twenty cubits: so that the Holy of Holies was still a perfect cube, but was now doubled to twenty by twenty by twenty cubits. Turning now right to the end of the Bible, to the twenty-first chapter of the Apocalypse, where the celestial city is described—"that great city, the holy Jerusalem, descending out of heaven from God"—we find that its shape and dimensions are thus given, in verse 16—"And the city lieth foursquare; and the length is as large as the breadth . . . twelve thousand furlongs. The length and the breadth and the height of it are equal."

What is the symbolic meaning wrapped up in all this?—for symbolic meaning there undoubtedly is. The answer is not far to seek. This figure with its breadth and length and depth or height all equal is, of course, the *cube*; and the cube, because of its elementary and absolute symmetry, was to the old-time Hebrews *the symbol of perfection*.

Now, in a flash, we get the meaning in the cubic dimensions of the Holy of Holies and of the Celestial City. They bespeak, in the one case, the perfection of Israel's God, and in the other, the perfection of that queen city in the consummation yet to be. And surely this is what Hebrew Paul has in mind when he speaks of "the breadth and length and depth and height" of the love of Christ! It is that symbol of the cube again! He is thinking of the glorious *perfection* of the love of Christ. Oh, this glorious, all-perfect love of God's dear Son! It matters not from whichever standpoint we view the love of Christ, its perfection flashes forth —whether we think of its expression toward the Father or toward us poor human sinners, whether we think of its immensity or its intensity, its eternity or its sublimity, its deathless strength or its exquisite tenderness, its fulness and passion or its purity and gentleness, its majesty or its humility, its profundity or its simplicity, its expression or its motive—in its breadth and length and depth and height it is perfection all-glorious!

> Oh, for this love let rocks and hills,
> Their lasting silence break,
> And all creation's harmonies
> The Saviour's praises speak!

Now the love of Christ finds its crowning expression in the
Cross; but besides this, we find that the very circumstances of
our Saviour's crucifixion most strikingly *illustrate* the breadth
and length and depth and height of His love.

First, we are told that the superscription of His accusation
affixed to the Cross was written "in Hebrew and Greek and
Latin." These three languages symbolically embrace the entire
race. Here is the language of religion (Hebrew), of culture (Greek),
and of Law (Latin, or Roman). These three languages comprehended the whole of the ancient civilised world. Moreover, they
represent the characteristic types of men in all generations.
They reach out to all points of the compass, and bespeak the
universality of the Redeemer's love. Here, then, in this trilingual
superscription, we see the *BREADTH*. The wide-flung arms on
that wondrous Cross welcome the whole world.

Aye, but stand before that Cross again, and hear the Saviour's
anguished cry—"My God, my God, why hast thou forsaken me?"
Never can we know the utter suffering of that awful hour, or
sound the deeps of that inconceivable woe when the Father
Himself withdrew from the forsaken Son of His bosom. We can
but dimly discern that Christ's substitutionary identification with
man's sin somehow involved that He must know the darkness
of the Divine wrath, that He must in some deep and awful way
"taste death," and that even the Father must turn from Him
as He hung there—"made to be sin for us, who knew no sin,
that we might be made the righteousness of God in Him" (2 Cor.
v. 21). Surely that heart-rending cry, "My God, my God, why
hast Thou forsaken me?" measures the *LENGTH* to which the
Divine love would go, to save our souls and win the love of our
poor hearts.

But linger by that Cross a little longer. It stands between
two other crosses, for the Holy One of Israel is "numbered with
the transgressors," and dies between two thieves. Likely enough

a record of unmentionably vile crime lies behind these two wretches as now, in their last, pain-racked moments on earth, they hang suspended over the dark pit of hell: but one of them has broken down into genuine contrition. The fountains of his heart have become unsealed, and his tears have washed away his defiant curses. Yea more, through his tears he has seen in that central Sufferer what the proud, unseeing eyes of Israel's leaders have failed to see. He has recognised—so indeed it would seem—Israel's Messiah and the world's Saviour; and he cries out with all but his last breath—"Lord remember me when Thou comest into Thy kingdom!" And can the Saviour's love reach down low enough to lay hold even of this polluted son of evil? Hear His word—"Verily, I say unto thee, To-day shalt thou be with Me in paradise"! Behold the *DEPTH* to which the Saviour's love can reach, and the *HEIGHT* to which it can lift even such an one as the dying thief!

Truly, the Cross itself is the greatest illustration—as it is the greatest expression—of the breadth and length and depth and height of the love of Christ.

> The love that Jesus had for me,
> To suffer on the cruel tree,
> That I a ransomed soul might be,
>   Is more than tongue can tell.

BY WAY OF APPLICATION

But we must never separate the love of Christ from that of the Father, for, as the apostle tells us, "God was *in* Christ, reconciling the world unto Himself." The nails that were hammered through the Saviour's hands were driven into the Father's heart. The spear that rent the Saviour's side left its mark in the Father's bosom. The Father suffered both with and in the Son. In the breadth and length and depth and height of the love of Christ we are but beholding the measureless dimensions of the Father's own love for us.

And what is the meaning of it all? What is the meaning of this wonderful love of God, and of that never-to-be-forgotten Cross? It is this:

"THAT WHOSOEVER BELIEVETH IN HIM SHOULD NOT PERISH, BUT HAVE EVERLASTING LIFE."

It means that despite our hell-deserving sin, the great Creator-Father's heart yearns over us, and that although, in His absolute justice, the sovereign Ruler of the universe could not allow human sin to go unpunished, He has nevertheless provided, at infinite cost, a way of salvation for us from the pains and chains of our sin. It means that the eternal Son of God left Heaven's throne for Calvary's Cross and became our Substitute, bearing our penalty and guilt, and thus removing our black load. Yes, it means that there is now a Gospel to preach, which says:

"THAT WHOSOEVER BELIEVETH IN HIM SHOULD NOT PERISH, BUT HAVE EVERLASTING LIFE."

Turn back again, just for a moment, to Paul's words—"breadth and length and depth and height." Note the order here. Breadth comes first, then length, then depth, and lastly height. The pen of inspiration is clearly guided in observing this order. Change the order and you spoil the sequence. When we hear of such wonderful love as the love of God in Christ, what is the first thing we wish to know? Why, surely, we each want to know —"Does it include *me*?" In other words, we are asking how *broad* it is. Hence, Paul puts "breadth" first. And *does* the love of God in Christ take you and me in? Thank God it does; for the text says: "God so loved the *world* . . . that *whosoever*." I think the best definition I ever heard of that term "Whosoever" came from a Northampton newspaper boy. I was trying to show him that God had a special place in His great big heart all for *him*, and asked him if he knew what "Whosoever" meant. He replied: "Well, sir, you see it sort o' means everybody else —and *me*." It was a priceless answer; and it is pricelessly true. Most of us persist in vaguely relating the word to "everybody else," leaving out the "and *me*." Oh, my friend, if you will hear it, without the shadow of a doubt you are included in the saving love of God, and may become eternally saved by receiving the Saviour.

But when we are convinced about the breadth of God's love we want to know about the *length*. We have seen the length to which it would go to provide salvation; but what of its length in the sense of *duration*? How long will it last? If I trust myself to Christ, will His love wane, and finally cease, as my unworthiness becomes more and more exposed? This is God's answer: "Neither death nor life, nor angels nor principalities nor powers, nor things present nor things to come, nor height nor depth nor any other thing created, shall be able to separate us from the love of God which is in Christ Jesus our Lord " (Rom. viii. 38–9).

And finally, what of the *depth* and the *height*? "Ah, I have sinned till I am beyond redemption!" exclaims someone. "Maybe I have not sinned so vulgarly as some others; but I have sinned against special light and peculiar privileges, and have been really more sinful than many a murderer or blasphemer or drunkard. Can the love of God reach down even to me?" My brother, thank God for the sense of sin and need He has given you, and then let that dying thief of long ago tell you that the love which brought the holy Son of God to Calvary can reach down to the very gate of hell, and lift upwards to the very bliss of Paradise! It is true, utterly true:

"THAT WHOSOEVER BELIEVETH IN HIM SHOULD NOT PERISH, BUT HAVE EVERLASTING LIFE."

Oh, friend, look well at those wonderful words. Nay, more— look to that Cross and to that glorious Saviour. By turning from sin, and simply resting in complete reliance upon Him, become even now one of God's forgiven and redeemed children!

THE DIVINE SONSHIP

You must make up your mind along which of two ways
you are going to look for the explanation of Christianity.
Are you going to say that the Christian faith made
Christ or that Christ made the Christian faith? I mean,
are you going to take the view that historically Jesus
was of not more than humanly comprehensible stature,
but that His early disciples and apologists raised His
figure to a height of heroism, idealism, supernaturalism,
divinity, till they created the picture of the evangelic
tradition and the Church's faith; or, on the other hand,
the view that there really and historically was in Jesus,
as He actually existed, what originated and necessitated
all this for those who thought out and did justice to the
fact of Christ? It seems to me to involve an historical
paradox amounting to an impossibility that if, as a matter
of fact, Jesus was but a man among men, His primitive
apologists could ever have made Him into *the* Man for all
time. They could never have done it unless Jesus really
was what they represented Him to be.

P. Carnegie Simpson

THE DIVINE SONSHIP

"He gave His only begotten Son"—John iii. 16.

"HE GAVE His only begotten Son." In these words we clearly see *the Divine sonship of Christ.* This title, "His only begotten Son," implies the absolute deity of Christ. As Canon Liddon says, "The epithet 'only-begotten' means, not merely that God had no other such Son, but that His only begotten Son is, in virtue of this sonship, a partaker of that incommunicable and imperishable Essence which is sundered from all created life by an impassable chasm."

In these opening chapters of John, there are two profoundly expressive terms used of Christ, which together declare His real deity beyond all reasonable doubt. He is the *"Word"* and He is the *"Son."* These two metaphors supplement and protect each other. Taken separately, they might lead divergent thinkers to widely different and equally erroneous conceptions of Christ; but when they are taken together, each corrects the possible misuse of the other.

To think of Christ only as the "Word" might suggest merely an impersonal quality or faculty in God. To think of Christ only as the "Son" might limit us to the conception of a personal yet created being. But the two terms combined give us the full truth, and at the same time guard us from error. See how this is so. Christ is the "Word" (*Logos* = Word, Thought, Reason); but the Word, being also the "Son" cannot be merely an impersonal or abstract quality. Christ is the "Son"; but the Son, being also the "Word," cannot be a created being, and therefore of more recent origin than the Father, for it is impossible to think of the Father as ever being without that eternal Word, or Thought, or Reason, which is the Son. As Dr. Liddon says, these two metaphors together "exhibit Christ before His

49

incarnation as at once personally distinct from, and yet equal with, the Father."

Some years ago a Christian minister was preaching in a Midland town, when he was interrupted by a man in the audience who loudly challenged the preacher's emphasis on the deity of Christ. As the interrupter was insistent, the preacher felt obliged to address him directly for a moment, telling him that if he really wished to ask a serious question he could do so, on the understanding that there were no more interruptions from him. The man proved to be a "Millennial Dawnist"; and this was his objection: "You say that Jesus Christ is the eternal Son of God, and co-equal with the eternal Father; but He cannot be, for if He be God's *Son* He cannot be as old as the Father, since no son is as old as his father; and if Christ is not as old as the Father, then He is not eternal; and if He is not eternal, then He cannot be God, as you say He is." What would the preacher say to *that*? Well, he paused for a moment, and then gave this devastating reply: "Out of your own mouth will I condemn you. You yourself have just called God the eternal Father. Does it not strike you that God can only be the eternal Father by having an eternal Son? Eternal fatherhood demands eternal sonship. Moreover, you have said that Christ, the Son, cannot be as old as the Father because no son is as old as his father, and that Christ, therefore, cannot be eternal. You are wrong there too, for, strictly speaking, no father, as such, is older than his son, and no son is younger than his father. When did my own father begin to be my father? He began to be my father at the very same moment that I became his son. He is therefore exactly as old as a father as I am as a son! The very terms 'Father' and 'Son,' as used of the Godhead, imply co-equality in nature, and co-eternalness." There were no further interruptions!—and we can leave the preacher's reply to make its own impression.

There are very few people who seem to realise how much we lose if we reduce Christ to the Unitarian level of the Modernist and the new-fangled heretical sects which pester us to-day. Three vital facts, especially, we should bear in mind, which I will here mention. If Christ be not God, there is (1) no revelation of Divine love, (2) no atonement for sin, (3) no real Saviourhood.

A CREATURE-CHRIST NO LOVE-GIFT

First, if Christ is not Divine, in the absolute sense of the word, then *God's gift of Christ is not an expression of His love.* If Christ is a mere creature, it cost God nothing to give Him. The whole point about John iii. 16, with its "God *so* loved," is that God, in giving "His only begotten Son," did that which was unspeakably costly to Himself; but if His gift was that of a mere creature, it was not in the least costly to Himself. The very heart is plucked out of the Gospel. In fact there is no Gospel at all. The one decisive demonstration of the love of God is gone. The difference between a worm and an archangel, between an insect and a seraph, between the lowest of all created beings and the highest, is little, is nothing, compared with the measureless gulf between the highest of all created beings and— *God.*

That God should give a mere creature, whether high or low, is no expression of amazing love. It is more like a multi-multi-millionaire's tossing a coin to some poor beggar. Nay, worse; for other than being an expression of love, it is an act of strange cruelty that God should delegate one of His unfallen and innocent creatures to the bitter ordeal of that awful Cross and agony which are now forever identified with human sin. The lustre dies off from John iii. 16 and its kindred texts. They become pathetically meaningless. "God so loved the world that He gave —an angel, a seraph, a creature of high rank." What does any such gift as these convey of Divine love? Nothing! The glory of the Gospel lies in the fathomless mystery that for our sakes God gave up, to the shame and suffering of Calvary, One who was and is eternally the Son of His bosom and the delight of His heart.

A CREATURE-CHRIST NO SAVIOUR

Second, if Christ is not Divine, in the outright sense, then *there is no atonement for human sin.* All those verses in the New Testament which speak of Christ's death as an expiation and putting away of sin, or as a propitiation and satisfaction for sin, are merely foundationless theory. The so-called Atonement is a delusion and not a reality; for no mere creature could possibly make atonement for the sin of the human race, no, not even the highest of the highest, the *excelsus* of the creatures. No created being, however exalted, possesses that which he can offer in the behalf of man. Every created intelligence, however lofty, must confess: "All that I am, God made me. All that I have, God gave me. I live because He sustains me. Nothing that I am or have is attributable to self-origination. I am therefore not the independent proprietor of my own being. In the sum-totality of my being I am the property of Another, who made me, who gives me life, and in whom I live and move and have my being." Therefore, since all creatures are the property of the Creator, no mere creature could possibly offer that which might constitute an atonement for human sin. Only One who is Divine can do that. Or we may put it this way, that a created—and there-fore *finite*—being could not possibly exhaust the *infinite* suffering involved in the penalty of human sin. Only a Divine—and therefore *infinite*—Being could do that. If, therefore, Christ is not really Divine, then His death is neither an expiation of sin nor an atonement for man.

A CREATURE-CHRIST NOT OMNIPRESENT

Third, if Christ is anything less than God, then *Christ's presence with and within His people is an empty imagination*. All those passages in the New Testament which speak of the risen Christ as being present with all His people at all times and in all places, are rendered absurd. His great assurance—"Lo, I am with you alway, even unto the end of the age," is nothing but the vain fancy of a credulous optimism. Anyone can see this; for if Christ be not Divine, then He does not possess the Divine attri-butes; and, in particular, He does not possess the Divine attribute of *omnipresence*, the quality of being simultaneously present everywhere; so that He cannot be everywhere with His people, much less can He actually indwell them. He is limited, local, in one place, and only one, at any given time.

Not long ago a Rutherford-ite, or Millennial Dawn emissary,

came to my door, selling his books. He called himself one of the "Footstep Followers of Jesus," and thought to interest me in his pseudo-gospel. As is usual with such persons, he sought to dodge straight questions by plausible ambiguity, using the well-known Christian names and terms with a meaning quite different from the generally accepted meaning. When I asked him if he believed in Jesus Christ as the Son of God, he replied that Jesus is *a* son of God. When I repeated the question as to whether he believed in Him as *the* Son of God, he hesitated, and then rather falteringly agreed that we might call Him even *the* Son of God. Not being sure of the man's sinceritv, however, I put the further question—"Do you believe, then, that the Lord Jesus Christ is actually *God, the Son?*"—and to this he replied an immediate "No." He had known all the time what I was getting at, and had known all the time what he believed, or rather did *not* believe, about the Lord Jesus, but had sought to deceive by a smoke-screen of ambiguousness.

My own experience is that this mark of deceit—for such it undoubtedly is—characterises not only Millennial Dawnism, but Christian Science (so-called), and others of our present-day new-fangled heterodoxies. However, to keep to this man at my door—I asked him: "If your Christ is not God, where is He?" He seemed at little uncertain how to reply, and then jerked out: "He is now in heaven." To this I rejoined: "Ah, well, then, you'll not do much business at *my* door, for *your* gospel isn't as good as mine. *Your* Christ is far, far, far away in a distant sky: *my* Christ is both on the throne of glory and at the same time *here with me*, at the doorstep, and *in my heart*; for He is God." Oh, how precious has the thought of the Saviour's presence and indwelling been to His people in every time and place! Yet such a presence and indwelling is a mere fiction if Christ be not indeed God the Son.

There are other tragic losses befall us if Christ be not intrinsically Divine, as, for instance, that His teaching becomes shorn of its absolute authority and finality; but we will not tarry further; for the three considerations which we have just discussed are enough in themselves. It is with a sense of relief that we turn back again to our grand old text, John iii. 16, convinced that, by its very wording, it accords Divine uniqueness to Christ, when it says, "For God so loved the world, that He gave His *ONLY BEGOTTEN SON*."

THE GOD-MAN SAVIOUR

Oh, what a Saviour this is! Because He is truly human and at the same time absolutely Divine, He spans the gulf between sinful man and the all-holy God. None other could do this. A Christ truly human yet not absolutely Divine would be a bridge from man's side of the gulf which could not reach *God's* side of it; while on the other hand, a Christ absolutely Divine yet not truly human would be a bridge from God's side of the gulf which could not reach *man's* side of it. In Jesus Christ, Son of God and Son of Man, the gulf is bridged. There is no other Saviour. Thank God, there is no *need* of any other; for this one-and-only Saviour is all-sufficient.

Because this Saviour is truly human—"bone of our bone and flesh of our flesh"—He is able to represent man to God; and because He is absolutely Divine—"very God of very God"—He is able to represent God to man. He becomes the Representative of both—of each to the other. In Him—the perfect Man and the Father's incarnate Coequal—God and men meet. He is the Middleman, or Mediator, even as the Scripture says—"There is one God, and one Mediator between God and men, the man Christ Jesus." Because He is the perfect Man He is an acceptable Substitute for man, on Calvary; and because He is also the incarnate Son of God He has the infinite capacity in Himself to exhaust the penalty due to man's sin. Thus, in Him, there is effected an at-one-ment between God and men.

Because He is truly man, and because on the Cross He took the place of the lowest sinner, He can reach down to the very lowest of sinners, and save them from the penalty and pollution and power of their sin; and because He is also God the Son, He can lift those whom He saves to the highest height of exaltation. If the Redeemer were merely a perfect man, then at best He could only lift us to His own level of humanity. Or if the Redeemer were an incarnate angel, then at best He could only lift us to the level of the angels. But the Redeemer is none other than the incarnate, crucified, and now risen Son of God Himself; and He can lift us up to the very throne of God, to share with Himself the highest heights of glory. Well may we sing: "Hallelujah, what a Saviour!"

This is our matchless Saviour. Oh that we prized Him, and preached Him, and praised Him as we ought! The deep and passionate resolve of every Christian heart should be:

> E'er since by faith I saw the stream
>   Thy flowing wounds supply,
> Redeeming love has been my theme,
>   And shall be till I die.

> Then, in a nobler, sweeter song,
>   I'll sing Thy power to save;
> With sinless heart and raptured tongue
>   In triumph o'er the grave.

Yes, this is the none-such Saviour Who gave Himself to redeem us, and who now lives to save us. This is the Saviour of whom it is written that "He is able to save them to the uttermost that come unto God by Him, seeing He ever liveth to make intercession for them."

Oh friend now hearing my word, have *you* accepted this Saviour? Are *you* among those whose names are written in the Lamb's book of life? Have *you* yet realised your vital interest in the Redeemer's blood? Have *you* yet found in Him the triple blessing of pardon for sin, and peace with God, and prospect of heaven? His heart melts with tenderness. His arms are wide to welcome you. As someone has well said, He is able to save "from the guttermost to the uttermost." He can save from the deepest deep of sin to the highest height of holiness, and to the utmost reach of eternity. He can save *you*. He waits to be gracious. He is at your very hand. He knocks at your heart's door. He gives His pledged word to enter where He is invited. Can you not trust Him? Will you not now receive Him? Why perish without Him? Why turn away, when by faith in Him you may be eternally saved? Yes, believe this, He waits to save *you*, and to save you *now*. This is how God's promise runs—"Believe on the Lord Jesus Christ, and thou shalt be saved." It is really true; for "God so loved the world, that He gave His only begotten Son, that whosoever believeth in *HIM* should not perish, but have everlasting life."

THE DIVINE FATHERHOOD

THE DIVINE FATHERHOOD

"He gave His only-begotten Son"—John iii. 16

WE ARE SPEAKING carefully when we say that these words open up to us the most profound and precious truth that the human mind can ever contemplate. What infinitude of meaning there is when we consider this Giver and this Gift! "Thanks be unto God for His unspeakable gift!" exclaims Paul as he thinks of Christ and the Cross. The more deeply we apprehend the meaning of Bethlehem and Calvary, the more we are obliged to fall back on that Pauline adjective, "unspeakable."

"Unspeakable." It was with care that Paul picked this adjective. There was none of that glib extravagance which characterises our popular use of adjectives today. It is the one adjective which fits. In the utter sense Christ is God's *"unspeakable"* gift. In these days we need to make war against gross exaggerations. There never was a time when superlatives were splashed around so prodigally as they now are over television and radio, in newspapers and magazines. During election time in Britain, as Mr. Churchill was approaching a certain town, a loudspeaker was blaring, "Here comes Winnie—watch the third car; the greatest statesman in the world; the greatest man on earth." Just about the same time, *Pravda* was saying of Stalin, "He stands on a pinnacle never reached before. He is the greatest general of all nations"; and Moscow radio was shouting him round as "the greatest military genius of all time" who "saved freedom and the world."

"Unspeakable." There is nothing of such gaudy salesmanship when the writers of our New Testament resort to superlatives. I imagine Paul as pausing and pondering before he picked and penned that word, "unspeakable," for it is the one and only place in the New Testament where that Greek word occurs.

This is a gift of such staggering immensity and infinite glory
that language breaks down. Christ, as the Father's gift, is a
sheer divine wonder. He is the supreme superlative. He is utterly
"*unspeakable.*" And why? For three reasons. First, because of
who He is. Second, because of what He did. Third, because of
the *results* from what He did. He has brought us free, full, final
forgiveness for our sins; reconciliation with God; justification
through imputed righteousness; absolution from guilt; new spiritual life; restored sonship in the family of God; with the pledge
of immortality and eternal glory!

"*Unspeakable.*" Oh, the unspeakableness indeed of such a
gift! What food is to the starving; what water is to the thirsting;
what liberation is to the slave; what riches are to the poverty-
stricken; what relief is to the beleaguered; what release is to the
condemned prisoner; what healing is to the diseased and dying;
what all these are, and much more, is Jesus Christ, Son of God,
Saviour of men. Yes, language breaks down; He is "*unspeakable.*"

With this Pauline adjective in mind, then, pause again at
John iii. 16, and reflect on the great *Giver:* "He gave His only-
begotten Son." If we think penetratively, it will not be long
before we find ourselves uniting with Paul in his exclamation of
thankful wonder.

A CROWNING POINT OF REVELATION

To begin with, we see here, in implication, the relationship
of *fatherhood* attributed to Him whom we distinguish as the
First Person in the eternal Triunity; for if He gave His "only-
begotten *Son*," then it follows (quite apart from whether we can
grasp the mystery of it or not) that He sustains the relationship
of *Father*. Now God the Father sustains this relationship of
fatherhood in a *unique* way towards Christ; but He has revealed
Himself, also, as Father to *ourselves*: and this revelation of His
fatherhood is the crowning point of Biblical revelation regarding
the divine relationship to us.

It is at once meaningful that the Biblical revelation, considered as a whole, presents first the sovereign *power* of God—
as seen in the creation, the Flood, the Babel dispersion, the

Exodus; next the inviolable *holiness* of God—as seen in the Mosaic Law, and the subsequent divine dealings with Israel, notably through the Hebrew prophets; and next the sublime *love* of God—as seen culminatively in the Gospel of Christ. The truth is at once apparent that the revelation of the *love* of God must be safeguarded by a due recognition of His all-disposing power and utter holiness.

The characteristic word for God, on the lips of Jesus, is "Father"; but let it be ever remembered that *not until* Jesus came, as the completive revelation of God, was the divine fatherhood given this prominence. The truth of the divine fatherhood is not safe for fallen man to possess without the earlier revelation of God's supreme power and awe-inspiring holiness. In nothing is the divine wisdom more clearly observable than in this progressive tuition, and the postponed disclosure of the heavenly fatherhood. In ancient religions where there has been no such safeguard as that which we see in the Biblical revelation, no conception is less ethical than that of divine fatherhood, with the result that the whole character of the deity is correspondingly degraded. Such are the moral necessities of the case, that it is only safe for man to say, "Our Father which art in heaven,"when he has learned immediately to add,"Hallowed by Thy name." One of the big faults in certain schools of modern theology is the mental divorcing of the divine love and fatherhood from the preparatory Biblical emphasis on the divine transcendence and sin-abhorring holiness. It is unwholesome and dangerous.

THE ULTIMATE RELATIONSHIP

Fatherhood is not the only relationship which God sustains to us. He is Creator, King, Judge, Father, and more, all in one. But the other relationships lose meaning apart from the fatherhood. The divine creatorship, without fatherhood, loses its highest motives and loftiest ends. Did God create only to provide existence? The divine kingship, likewise, apart from fatherhood, loses its worthiest authority and weightiest influence. Did God create only to rule? The divine judgeship, apart from the fatherhood, equally loses its purest compulsion and truest safeguard. Did God create only to judge? The fatherhood is surely the basal, ultimate, inclusive relationship. He is not merely Creator, King, Judge. He did not create merely to sustain, to govern, to judge. There is a motive, an end, and a method toward the realising of that end, which proceed from His fatherhood. The fatherhood of God is not subordinate to, or comprehended by, His other relationships as Creator, King, Judge; nay, on the contrary, those other relationships are subordinate to, and comprehended in, the fatherhood: they are the expression of, and are conditioned by, the fatherhood. The fatherhood includes kingship; for fatherhood minus kingship is incompletely manifested. The fatherhood also includes the legislative and judical; for its vigilance of love involves its inviolable maintenance of those laws which condition the well-being of the family. God has willed into existence, out of His own life, creatures who are "in His own likeness," living and moving and having their being in Him, yet having distinct personal consciousness and volitional individuality. In this movement of God, the motive is love, the end is fellowship; and the method toward the realising of that end is the education of the family; all of which have their ground in, and are the expression of, the divine *fatherhood*.

FATHERHOOD AND ATONEMENT

All this, however, raises a stupendous question: If God is thus the heavenly Father, why should the Atonement be necessary? It has often been asked: "Does fatherhood, either human or divine, require a 'satisfaction' before it will forgive?"—and many have replied, "No." The old Socinian argument was that if any earthly father, worthy of the name, will forgive his child for wrongs done, without first demanding a "satisfaction," surely the compassion of the heavenly Father cannot be less. Nay, as we would expect, His many invitations to sinners, contained in the Scriptures, show that His compassion far excels that of earthly fathers.

It is surprising and disappointing to find the Puritan theologians, and even later evangelical princes like R. W. Dale, accepting this paltry idea of a fatherhood shorn of all its more virile qualities, as representing the fatherhood of God; and it is pathetic to find them—instead of repudiating such an inadequate conception of fatherhood—resorting to the reply that the Atonement is made necessary by one of those sterner relationships which God sustains to men, i.e. His being King, or Moral Governor, and Judge, as well as Father—as though the different acts of God spring from His different relationships, so that at one time He is acting as Judge, at another time as King, and at another time as Father.

The late Dr. J. Scott Lidgett aptly commented:"The relationship of God to man is a unique and living whole. Each purpose and act of God towards men is founded upon the whole of His nature and the whole of His relationships, not upon a part of them. It is less possible for the heavenly Father to divest Himself of fatherhood in any of His dealings with men than for an earthly father to do so in his dealings with his child. Different aspects and functions of His fatherhood may, no doubt, be abstracted from the whole, for purposes of thought. We may set, for example, in the forefront for the moment, His legislative or His governmental or His judical activity; but we must not suppose that the entire action of God proceeds from, or is explained by, any one of those aspects or functions in severance from His fatherhood which is over, in, and through them all."

The true reply to those who say that the fatherhood of God does away with the necessity for the Atonement is that *they are arguing from a conception of fatherhood which is utterly inadequate*, a conception of fatherhood, moreover, which is far removed from that which is taught by our Lord Jesus. In dealing with a rebellious child, a conscientious father must observe four sacred principles. First, he must act in such a way as does justice to his own character. Second, He must maintain the authority of his own will in and for the good of the whole family. Third, he must assert the sanctity of the law which has been broken. Fourth, he must act in such a way as to bring home to the child a penitent consciousness of wrong. Apply these four considerations to the heavenly Father in relation to us human creatures, and it will be seen at once that it is the very fatherhood of God, not merely His kingship or moral governorship, which necessitates the Atonement. And further, the more deeply we ponder the Cross of Christ, the more do we become convinced that there could be no other way whereby these four sacred principles of true fatherhood might be respected and vindicated in the divine dealings with mankind.

That Cross upholds the *character* of the divine Father; for it magnifies both His holiness and His love. Second, it exalts the *authority* as well as the beneficence of the Father's will; for our glorious Representative who hung there became "obedient unto death, even the death of the Cross." Third, it asserts and honours the sanctity of the *Law* which has been broken; for it is the means whereby full satisfaction is rendered. Fourth, it also brings home to our human hearts, as nothing else ever could, a *penitent sense of our sin*.

Yes, that Cross is a necessity of the divine fatherhood; but if the fatherhood of God necessitated it, thank God, the fatherhood also *provided* it. That is why it ever came to be written: "God so loved the world that He gave His only-begotten Son, that whosoever believeth in Him should not perish, but have everlasting life."

AN OLD TESTAMENT PICTURE

"He gave His only-begotten Son." Undoubtedly there is in these words an allusion to Abraham's offering up of Isaac. There is a similar allusion to Abraham in Romans viii. 32, where Paul says, "He that spared not His own Son, but delivered Him up for us all, how shall He not with Him also freely give us all things?" Every Jew knew and loved to tell of his great forefather, Abraham, who was willing to sacrifice even his only-begotten and well-beloved Isaac. Beyond any doubt, Abraham is a divinely fashioned forepicture of the great *heavenly* Father. We see the correspondence in eight ways.

(1) *In the uniqueness of his love for Isaac.* The unique circumstances connected with the promise and birth of Isaac made him the object of Abraham's tenderest love; so that he was with special emphasis, "Isaac whom thou lovest."

(2) *In the costliness of his sacrifice.* How this is underlined in the words, "Take now thy son, thine only son Isaac, whom thou lovest . . . and offer him!" How costly indeed, to sacrifice the dear son of his old age, in whom all his own hopes and all the divine promises were centred!

(3) *In his readiness to make the sacrifice.* Not one demur on Abraham's part is recorded, though Jehovah's strange and heart-breaking request must have contradicted everything which up to that point he had learned of Him and His ways.

(4) *In his preparation and foresight.* See Abraham, several days in advance of the ordeal, preparing the requisites for the offering; then on the third day lifting up his eyes and seeing the place "afar off." So was Calvary seen "afar off" and prepared for.

(5) *In his intense suffering.* How glad would Abraham have been to give his own life rather than his precious Isaac! His suffering was dual: that of his own heart in its loss, and that of sympathy with victim Isaac. So was it with the *heavenly* Father at Calvary.

(6) *In that his sacrifice revealed his heart.* It did so as nothing else could. In fact it is the supreme thing we know about him. Supremely it revealed his love to God (Gen. xxii. 12). So is Calvary the supreme unveiling of the heart of God. "Herein is love, not that we loved God, but that He loved us, and sent His Son to be the propitiation for our sins" (1 John iv. 10).

> Not even God a greater gift could give,
> Nor heaven itself a dearer boon impart;
> When Jesus came and died that I might live,
> God gave without reserve His very heart.

(7) *In that his sacrifice was in response to a call.* It was a voice from Heaven which called the patriarch to that costly altar (Gen. xxii. 1, 2). There was a divine necessity in it. Abraham could not have been led to the highest height of faith and fellowship, or have given such finally decisive evidence of love to God apart from it. Even so the heavenly Father's giving at Bethlehem and Calvary was in response to a call, not of heaven to earth, but of earth to heaven, a cry of human need and woe.

(8) *In that his sacrifice had wonderful beneficent results.* In the end, as we know, Abraham did not need actually to sacrifice Isaac. God did not desire that: but so far as Abraham's faith was concerned, the deed was as good as done; and God said that in consequence should "all nations of the earth be blessed" (Gen. xxii. 15-18). Even so, and immeasurably more so, is it with the beneficent results of the *heavenly* Father's yielding up of the only-begotten Son. Read Revelation vii. 9-17, which tells of that multitude which "no man could number"—redeemed, regenerated, sanctified, glorified, in robes of sinless purity, and waving palms of eternal victory! Yes, read it again, and marvel again at the wonderful consequences of "God so loved that He gave . . . ."

WHAT IT INVOLVED

"He gave His only-begotten Son." That word, "gave," has in it the force of "gave *up*." As an old commentator says, God gave His Son, not only *to* the world, but *for* it. That meant the birth in the cattle shed at Bethlehem, the struggle with poverty at Nazareth, the carpenter's bench, the being "tempted in all points like as we are," the suffering of reproach and the being "acquainted with grief," the shame and the spitting, the purple robe and the crown of thorns, the iron spikes and the deadly spear, the awful darkness and the "tasting of death." Oh, there is titanic meaning in Paul's words, "He *spared not* His own Son."

Was ever a gift like the Saviour given? He leaves the bosom of the eternal Father and comes to the bosom of an earthly mother. The Son of God becomes the Son of Mary. The Infinite becomes an infant. He who holds the worlds in His arms is held in the arms of a frail woman. He whose garment is space, whose house is the universe, whose chariots are the clouds, and whose diadems are the stars, is wrapped in swaddling bands, and laid in a manger. He leaves the songs of the angels, for the gibes and taunts of wicked crucifiers. He leaves the palace-beautiful of heaven for the stable and the work-bench, and the having "not where to lay His head." He lays aside His celestial insignia, for the peasant dress and the purple robe of ridicule. He puts aside His sceptre of universal sovereignty, for the reed of mock royalty in Pilate's hall. He leaves the very throne of heaven, for that cross outside the city wall. He who is the Prince of Life bows His head in death. He who is without sin becomes the Sinbearer. The Christ of God becomes the Crucified. He who is the Father's delight becomes the God-forsaken. He who lit the stars lies in the dust. He comes, He toils, He hungers and thirsts, He weeps, He suffers, He bleeds and dies; He redeemingly agonizes in a depthless, boundless infinity of suffering which only His infinite *capacity* for suffering could experience; for "God SO loved the world that He GAVE UP His only-begotten Son."

Oh, how different is God's giving from men's! In all too many instances men's giving is for self-advantage; their giving is a subtle form of getting; but God gives out of pure compassion and benevolence. Men's giving can be only to a certain extent; but God's is without limit. Men's giving is usually in response to the urgent cries of the worthy for help; but God gives to those who neither realise their need nor appreciate His gift. Men's giving is usually to friends; but God gives His Gift of gifts to those who are alienated and rebellious; for as the Scripture says, "In due time, Christ died for the *ungodly*," and again, "When we were *enemies* we were reconciled to God by the death of His Son" (Rom. v. 8 & vi. 10). Contemplating it all, the poet, Edward Young, in his *Night Thoughts*, writes,

> And what is this?—survey the wondrous cure;
> And at each step let higher wonder rise!
> A pardon bought with blood; with blood divine!
> With blood divine of Him I made my foe!—
> Persisted to provoke, though woo'd and awed,
> Blessed and chastised, a flagrant rebel still!
> A rebel, 'neath the thunders of His throne;
> Nor I alone; a rebel universe;
> My species up in arms, not one exempt!
> Yet for the foulest of the foul He dies,
> As if our race were held of highest rank,
> And Godhead dearer as more kind to man!
> Oh, what a scale of miracles is here!—
> Its lowest round high planted in the skies;
> Its towering summit lost beyond the thought
>   Of man or angel.

THE ALL-INCLUSIVE GIFT

In giving Christ, God gives us all things *in* Him. Do we need forgiveness? God does not offer us forgiveness as a thing by itself. If we would receive a heavenly Father's forgiveness for all our sins, we must receive Jesus Christ Himself, for God's forgiveness comes to us *only* but *fully* in *Him*. Do we seek cleansing? Peace with God? The assurance of salvation? The gift of eternal life? Power to overcome evil habits and strong temptation? Courage to confess the Saviour before men? Spiritual equipment for service? Fellowship with God? Joy and comfort and hope? A dwelling in the "Father's house," and an inheritance among "them that are sanctified"? Not one of these divine blessings is given to us as a thing by itself. They are all included in the one comprehensive gift of the "only-begotten Son."

Friend, are *you* seeking pardon, cleansing, peace, power, assurance, eternal life, joy, comfort, hope, and a blessed hereafter? Do not seek them merely as a number of blessings which you feel you need. See in Jesus *ALL* that poor sinners can ever need for their present and continuous salvation and everlasting well-being. God *freely* gives us all things *IN HIM*. To possess Him is to possess all. Receive *HIM*.

"He *gave* His only-begotten Son." Yes, Christ is a *gift*. What is our normal response to a gift? Do we pay for it? Do we work for it? Do we beg for it? Do we needlessly wait for it? No; we just take it, and it is ours. If then Jesus is God's gift to us, our proper response is simply and gratefully to receive Him; and it is in doing just this that we become eternally saved *in Him*.

What a sad thing it is that millions of people treat God's gift with an unintelligent artificiality such as they would never display toward any other precious gift! Although in clear language the old Book tells us that the Saviour is the "gift of God," and that He may be savingly received by the simplest among us, men and women try to *pay* for salvation by supposed merit of character; or they try to *earn* it by energetic "good works" or so-called religious service; or they pray and wait and weep for it through days and nights of anxious concern about their eternal destiny. What folly, what tragedy, what stupidity it all is! If a friend offers me a gift, how do I show him that I really believe he is giving it to me? Why, by simply and gratefully taking it, of course. If I should start profusely thanking my friend, or wordily praising him for his kindness, or carefully explaining that his gift is exactly what I am needing, or assuring him that it will be most useful; if I should do all these things most volubly, yet not take the proffered gift, my friend would either say or think, "Well, in spite of all your thanking and explaining and praising and assuring, you do not honestly believe that I am really giving you this thing, or you would *take* it." Yes, taking is the simple but vital evidence of believing. The great heavenly Father still offers the "unspeakable Gift," and the Bible promise reads, "Whosoever will, let him take . . . ." Oh, for a simple enough faith to *take* and thereby to *prove!*

"He gave His only-begotten Son." In this, then, see supremely the heavenly Father's *love*. God does not love because Christ died. Christ died because love gave. See also the heavenly Father's *grace*; for a gift is something offered without obligation. See further the heavenly Father's *concern*. If He would allow His eternal Son to undergo the humiliation, the stark agony, and depthless woe of Calvary, how great must be His concern to save us!—and how awful must be that ages-long Gehenna from which He would fain rescue us!

A gift may be either received or *refused*. It is never forced upon an intended receiver, or it ceases to be a gift in the real sense of the word. Not even in the giving of salvation will God violate the responsible freedom of the human will. None of those who finally perish will be able to allege that salvation was not made free enough. Nay, it is a "*gift*"! God grant that each one of us may simply, truly *receive*, and then *rejoice* in the proven reality of salvation.

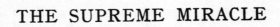
THE SUPREME MIRACLE

Two gentlemen were once disputing on the divinity of Christ. One of them, who argued against it, said, "If it were true, it certainly would have been expressed in more clear and unequivocal terms." "Well," said the other, "admitting that you believed it, were you authorised to teach it and allowed to use your own language, how would you express the doctrine to make it indubitable?" "I would say," replied he, "that Jesus Christ is *the true God*." "You are very happy," replied the other, "in the choice of your words, for you have happened to hit upon the very words of inspiration. St. John, speaking of the Son, says, 'This is THE TRUE GOD, and Eternal Life!'"

Anon

THE SUPREME MIRACLE

"He gave His only begotten Son"—John iii. 16.

"HE GAVE His only begotten Son." We have seen how these words imply the Divine fatherhood, and the Divine sonship. Are we not right in saying that they also imply *the reality of the Incarnation?* The words: "His only begotten Son" refer to Jesus Christ, a real and historical Person. They tell us that "The Word became flesh, and dwelt among us."

THE THEOPHANIES

Running through the Old Testament there is a remarkable chain of instances in which God communicates in visible form with men. These are known theologically as the "Theophanies" (Greek, *Theos*, God; with *Phainomai*, I appear); and the more we reflect on these, the more clearly do we perceive them to have been appearings of the Son of God long before the time when He became actually incarnate by the miracle of Bethlehem.

For instance, in Genesis xviii we read of the "three men" who visited Abraham, at Mamre. One of them is immediately singled out and addressed by Abraham as "my Lord" (verse 3). This One is the spokesman; and He speaks as being Divine, promising the birth of Isaac (verses 9–14). He is clearly distinguished from the two "angels," and is actually called "Jehovah" (verses 17, 20, 22, 26, 33). It is with Him that Abraham intercedes for Sodom; and it is by Him that retribution is afterward executed on the wicked city. There is surely here the unfaltering implication of the Divine presence in visible form.

Again and again there are the appearances of One who bears the title, "the Angel of Jehovah," but who speaks and acts as being actually one with God. When Hagar fled from Sarah

(Gen. xvi), it was the Angel of Jehovah who appeared to her in the wilderness, and spoke words which it is only the prerogative of God to speak.—"*I* will multiply thy seed exceedingly, that it shall not be numbered for multitude"; and Hagar named that place: "Thou God seest me." Later, when Abraham lifts the knife to slay his son (Gen. xxii), it is the Angel of the Lord who calls from heaven, and says: "Lay not thine hand upon the lad, neither do thou anything unto him: for now I know that thou fearest God, seeing thou hast not withheld thy son, thine only son, from *Me*" (thus actually identifying Himself with God).

In Genesis xxviii we have the story of Jacob's flight from Esau, and of his dream at Bethel. In his dream he sees the ladder from earth to heaven, with the angels of God ascending and descending upon it; while above it Jehovah Himself stands, and says: "I am Jehovah, God of Abraham thy father, and the God of Isaac; the land whereon thou liest, to thee will I give it, and to thy seed. . . ." Turning over to chapter xxxi, we find the *Angel* saying to Jacob: "*I am* the God of Bethel"; thus clearly identifying Himself again with Jehovah. Then there is the strange account of the man who wrestled with Jacob until daybreak at the brook Jabbok, and of whom Jacob says, "I have seen God face to face" (Gen. xxxii. 30).

We pass on to the time of Moses. The third chapter of Exodus tells us that this "Angel of Jehovah" appears to Moses in the flaming bush of Horeb. But the Angel says: "*I am* the God of thy father Abraham, the God of Isaac, and the God of Jacob," thus clearly identifying Himself yet again with Jehovah (verse 6). One after another, the Angel of Jehovah appropriates the Divine attributes to Himself (verses 7-14). The very ground on which Moses stands is made holy by that awful Presence; and Moses must needs take off his shoes. We are told, moreover, that Moses hid his face, "for he was afraid to look upon God" (verse 6). Like those before him, to whom the Angel of Jehovah had appeared, Moses realised that he was in the presence of God Himself.

Passing over other instances, we find the Angel of Jehovah appearing to Gideon, in the time of the Judges (Judges vi). When He suddenly revealed Himself, He said: "*Jehovah* is with thee!"; and right through the account He is represented as being one with God Himself. Gideon recognises Him to be more than an angel, and exclaims, in fear of death: "Alas, O Lord God! because I have seen the Angel of Jehovah face to face." It is the same with Manoah and his wife (Judges xiii), when the Angel of Jehovah (also called "the Angel of God," verse 9) appears and preannounces the birth of Samson. Manoah recognises the presence of One who is more than an angel, and exclaims: "We shall surely die, because we have seen God." In verse 18 the Angel declares His name to be "Wonderful" (not "secret," as in our Authorised Version)—a name which is later used of Christ, in the prophecy of Isaiah ix. 6.

We need not mention other instances. The foregoing are sufficient to convince us that "the Angel of Jehovah" is none other than the pre-incarnate Son of God, revealing Himself in bodily form from time to time. Besides serving their immediate purpose, these appearances were, we believe, a means of preparing men's minds for the coming miracle of the Incarnation by which the Son of God should actually become one with the human race, as the Son of Man.

THEOPHANIES VERSUS INCARNATION

But there may be those who ask what is the difference between the Incarnation and these earlier appearances in bodily form. Were they not, for all practical purposes, the same? Why was there need for Christ to be born at Bethlehem? Could He not, with equal effectiveness, and far more simply, have occupied a human body created for the purpose? To ask that question is to miss the meaning of the Incarnation entirely and pathetically.

When Christ appeared to men in the Old Testament dispensation, by means of the so-called "Theophanies," He merely utilised some visible form which was prepared for the purpose of the moment, and which was discarded immediately afterward. But when, at Bethlehem, Christ entered our human life by the way of a real human birth, He was doing something far more than merely occupying a human form: for in that supreme miracle of history, He was verily taking to Himself our human *nature*: He was verily *becoming human*, to remain so forever, while at the same time necessarily remaining truly God; so that He is now "Jesus Christ"—Divine and human in one Person —"yesterday, and to-day, and forever." Oh, the mystery, the majesty, the mercy, of it!

There are learned thinkers who tell us that the idea of an Incarnation is inherent in the very Being of God and His relations to man. "If God be spirit and love, He must ever seek to reveal Himself to beings whom He has made capable of receiving such a revelation; and this consummates itself in the taking of manhood into God." An Incarnation is thus part of the process of the Divine life. But the Gospel message is not merely that of "*an*" Incarnation. Speaking carefully, we know no such thing as merely "an" Incarnation. There is only *THE* Incarnation. The marvel of the Incarnation is not barely that God became Man, but His becoming *THAT* Man—the Man of Nazareth and Galilee; the Man of Gethsemane and Calvary; the Man of the thorn-crown and the nail-prints and the spear-wound; the Man who cried out, amid the sweat and agony of the garden, "Oh, My Father, if it be possible, let this cup pass from Me: nevertheless, not My will, but Thine be done"; the Man who cried from the awful darkness, "My God, My God, why hast Thou forsaken Me?"—yea, the Man of the Easter morn, who has vanquished death, and brought life and immortality to light through the Gospel!—the Man who ascended from Olivet and now sits at the right hand of the Majesty on high, and is yet to return in the glory of the Father and with the hosts of the angels!—that Man who "ever liveth to make intercession for us," and who is "able to save to the uttermost all them that come unto God by Him"! Yes, the glory of the Incarnation is that God became *THAT* Man.

There are those who tell us that they cannot believe in the Incarnation because there is no other case of its kind in history. To these, of course, the simple answer is that there is no other case of its kind because there is no other Saviour. There is but the one Incarnation, because there is but the one Son of God. Note the words of our text again—"He gave His *only begotten* Son." "Neither is there salvation in any other: for there is none other name under heaven given among men whereby we must be saved" (Acts iv. 12).

> None other Lamb, none other Name,
>> None other hope in heaven or earth or sea;
>> None other hiding place from guilt and shame,
>>> None beside Thee.

"He gave His only begotten Son"—gave Him to take our very nature upon Himself, to share our life, to bear our sin, to suffer and bleed and die for us men and women, that we might be eternally saved. Oh, wonderful Giver! wonderful Gift! wonderful Gospel! Whenever we think carefully about the Cross, there are two. reflections which inevitably force themselves upon our minds: first, a salvation which cost such a price must indeed be a great salvation; and, second, a salvation which brings us such unspeakably precious and eternal blessings as those offered in the Gospel could only have been provided at infinite cost. The sin of man is a far more monstrous thing in God's universe than the holiest among the saints have ever yet realised: and the love of God, which suffered to redeem us, in the Christ of Calvary, is a far sublimer and profounder marvel than our dim understanding can know. But this we do know and rejoice in, that when the last and the worst has been said about human sin, the victory remains with Love. Both human sin and Divine love reach their climax at the Cross: but love triumphs. The love of God seizes upon the worst deed of man to express itself most graciously: and from that darkest of all tragedies comes that dearest of all truths which enables a man to say: "Praise God, I am *saved*!"

> O love of God! O sin of man!
>> In this dread act your strength is tried;
>> And victory remains with love:
>>> For He, our Lord, is crucified.

THE FORGOTTEN SAVIOUR

Have we ourselves believed on Jesus, to the salvation of our souls? or have we forgotten Him? A friend was trying to lead a young soldier to accept the Saviour. "There, lad, read the words for yourself," he said, pointing him to John iii. 16. The young soldier read slowly: "For God so loved the world, that He gave His"—and there he hesitated, stumbling a bit at the next word. Whether the light was bad or his sight defective I do not know, but he then continued—"He gave His only *FORGOTTEN* Son." The friend who was with him interrupted: "Stop, lad; you've got it all wrong," but at the same time realised that the soldier boy had stumbled on to an awful truth; for, with the many, God's only begotten Son, the Saviour, is in very deed God's *FORGOTTEN* Son!

Yes, that is the truth with millions of people to-day. It is not that there is open opposition or wilful rejection: but the Saviour is just—*forgotten.* We do not forget to eat or sleep, to see our friends, and to do a thousand other things; but we forget Him who is the expression of God's redeeming love, and without whom we must perish forever. Oh, let us pause and reflect on what we owe Him! Think again what that Cross means. John Ruskin says about a certain picture of the Crucifixion, by a great painter: "One must leave it to work its will on the spectator; for it is beyond all analysis and above all praise": but if such words may be used about a mere painting of the Crucifixion, how much truer are they of the Cross itself! Truly does the poet, Edward Young, say of it:

> There hangs all human hope; that nail supports
> The falling universe: that gone, we drop;
> Horror receives us, and the dismal wish
> Creation had been smothered in her birth.
> Darkness His curtain, and His bed the dust,
> When stars and suns are dust beneath His throne!
> In heaven itself can such indulgence dwell;
> Oh, what a groan was there! a groan not His;
> He seized our dreadful guilt; the load sustained;
> And heaved the mountain from a guilty world.
> A thousand worlds so bought were bought too dear!

Ah, such is the human heart, that it is easy to forget the Saviour. The love of money, of worldly pleasures, of fleshly indulgences, drugs the heart into insensitiveness to those better and sweeter joys which are to be found in Christ. Oh, let us throw off our torpor, and survey that wondrous Cross again! As it speaks to us of the fatherhood of God, and the saviourhood of Christ and the redeeming purpose of the Incarnation, let us gratefully appropriate it by faith, rejoicing to believe that Jesus hung there for each one of us.

> Father, Thine everlasting grace
>   Our scanty thought surpasses far.
> Thy heart still melts with tenderness;
>   Thine arms of love still open are—
> Returning sinners to receive
> That mercy they may taste, and live.
>
> O Love, Thou bottomless abyss,
>   My sins are swallowed up in Thee!
> Covered is my unrighteousness,
>   Nor spot of guilt remains on me;
> While Jesus' blood, through earth and skies,
> Mercy, free, boundless mercy, cries!

THE FOUNTAIN HEAD

It was said that history's noblest record of love was that of a heathen, Pylades, who forfeited his life to save his friend. But "God commendeth His love toward *us* in that while we were yet *sinners* Christ died for us." Calvary was the heart of the Eternal Love laid bare. Yes, unveil that Cross, and see. It was God's only mode of showing us His heart. It is infinite love labouring to reveal itself, agonising to utter its fulness. Apart from that act a boundless ocean of love would have remained forever shut up and unknown by God's creatures. But now it has found an ocean-channel. Beyond Calvary even God cannot go. Once and for ever the proof has been given—"God is love."

J. R. Macduff

THE FOUNTAIN HEAD

"For God so loved . . ."—John iii. 16.

LOOK at this gem of a text once again. Let its diamond facets flash their heavenly light into the mind. Run the eye over the precious words once more, and see the triple glory radiating from them—

GOD LOVES!
GOD GIVES!
GOD SAVES!

This is the most thrilling trinity of truths that ever fell on human ears or came to bless a suffering race. Yes, this is the gospel of John iii. 16—God loves, gives, saves! We can do nothing more profitable than turn our thoughts to this theme of themes again and again, feeding the mind on it, and enriching the life from it. We will think just here about the first of these three things, namely, that God *loves*; for this is the fountain-head, the first cause, the unkindled flame, from which all else comes.

LOVE, NOT PITY

"God so loved the world"—mark well that word "loved," for that is the word which gives warmth and colour to the whole verse. God's motive in giving His Son for us is not merely that of *pity*. How much poorer the verse sounds—how the warmth and glow die away from it—if we read it as "God so *pitied* the world"! How stiff and chill and unmelting it all becomes if we change that one word "loved" into "pitied"! Hell-deserving sinners though we are, and conscious of our ill-desert, we nevertheless yearn, not merely for God's pity, but for His reconciling love. We have grown very familiar with this thought of God's love for the world; but have we ever tried to sense what it would feel like to live in a world that God only pitied, and did not love?

I shall never forget the distress of a woman who once came to me and told me that after two or three years of married life she had found that her husband had never really loved her. He had been sorry for her in her circumstances of poverty, and had married her out of pity. I can still hear that woman's heartbroken cry—"Oh, I would sooner be married to the poorest of men, and be loved, than have the richest of men, and only be pitied!" No, it is not just pity that our hearts crave. Even the pity of God is not enough. We long to know that He feels towards us in love; and our text tells us that He *does* love us.

Often, as I look into the vast spaces of the sky, I thrill to think that the infinite One, who is everywhere immanent in the universe, *loves* me, all-unworthy though I am. What responses it awakes in my heart! How warm and homey the universe seems! How instinct with meaning and promise life becomes, despite the presence of pain and problem! What comfort there is in that all-pervading Presence! But if God only *pities* me, in the humiliating littleness of my creaturehood and the repellent disfigurement of my sinnership, how distant He becomes, and how cold the universe grows! Instead of penitently nestling in the great arms of a God who loves me, I immediately feel myself a fugitive from Him, vainly longing to be free from the need for His loveless pity. Thank God, John iii. 16 preaches a gospel, not merely of Divine pity, or mercy, or condescension, but of Divine *love*; for "God so *loved* the world."

BENEVOLENCE, NOT COMPLACENCE

Look at that word "loved" again. Does it really mean that the heart of the Eternal beats with such an emotion toward us? We scarcely dare think on the shameful record of human sin— the hatred and bitter strife, the murder and savage war, the boastful pride and defiance of God, the greed of gain and lust for power, the craze for godless pleasure, the sordid sensuality, the trail of slime throughout man's history, the condition of the world to-day, and the failures that mar even the best of lives.

It seems impossible for a holy God to love a world in which sin has wrought such ugliness.

Yet it remains true that God loves this world; and it will help us to grasp this if we understand the *kind* of love which God has for it. There are two kinds of love. There is the love of *complacence*—the love of some object because of its intrinsic excellence; and there is the love of *benevolence*—the love that loves for the sake of the good it can confer. God's love for this sinful world is not the love of complacence, the emotion of appreciative delight in an object of beauty; it is the love of magnanimous benevolence, the love which gives itself to lift the unlovely and undeserving into purity and beauty. It is the boundless, quenchless, age-to-age compassion of God for sinning, suffering men and women. Or, to keep close to the spirit of our text, it is that emotion toward us, in the heart of God, which most nearly corresponds to the tender solicitude, the yearning kindness, the patient, enduring, undying compassion of a *father* for his wayward and degenerate son. Yes, this love of God for us is a *fatherly* love.

Some time ago, a godless fellow was trying to argue an old woman out of her faith in the love of God. He made such little headway with the serene old saint that eventually he flared up into a rage, and became abusive. "Well, at any rate," he sneered, "even the Almighty Himself couldn't love *you*, for you're about the ugliest old woman in the world." In a soft voice, as though half speaking to God and half to herself, the old dame replied: "Ah well, it's good to know that my heavenly Father can love the ugliest old woman in the world." The dear old soul was absolutely true; for despite all the ugly wreckage made by sin in our lives—an ugly wreckage which is far uglier to the holy eye of God than any of us can realise—God still loves even the worst of us, with a love that never lets us go, and never gives us up.

RACIAL, NOT NATIONAL

Such, then, is the nature of God's love for us. But now look at the *sweep* of it—"God so loved the *world*." The word "world," as used here, is a synonym for mankind as a whole. God loves the entire human race, without distinction or exception.

The old-time Jews believed that God's love was a *national* love, for the Jew only. They looked upon themselves as heaven's favourites, and all others as Gentile "dogs." But without diminishing the love of God for Israel, the Gospel of Christ completely overrode this imaginary monopoly. The love which brought Jesus to Calvary recognises no such distinctions. The teaching of Israel's later prophets greatly broadened their people's outlook; yet for all that, Jewish Nicodemus must have felt strange minglings of wonder and surprise as he heard Jesus say: "For God so loved the *world*, that He gave His only begotten Son, that *whosoever* believeth in Him should not perish, but have everlasting life." What strange, new thoughts Nicodemus must have had as he walked home that night! Perhaps the words of Faber's hymn would have suited his feelings—

> For the love of God is broader
> 　Than the measures of man's mind;
> And the heart of the Eternal
> 　Is most wonderfully kind.

GENERAL, NOT PARTIAL

Some of the older Calvinistic theologians tried to argue that the love of God was a *partial* love—for the "elect" only. But we cannot tolerate any such supposed partiality with John iii. 16 before us. We cannot accept any such differentiation as a "general" love for one class, and a "particular" love for another. The relationship between Divine election and human free-will is a problem too big for finite minds to solve, and we shall certainly not dwell on it here; but be that problem what it may, if language can have honest meaning, the New Testament plainly declares the universality of the great Father's love. So far as the magnanimous invitations of the Gospel are concerned, the elect are "whosoever will," and the non-elect are "whosoever won't." In the Cross of Christ there is a redemptive value which is sufficient to save the whole race, for Christ is "the Lamb of God which beareth away the sin of the *world*." Admittedly, the redeeming power of that Cross only becomes *efficient* in "them

that believe," but this in no wise detracts from the fact that
it is *sufficient* for the whole world. That world-embracing Cross
is the provision of a world-embracing love; for "God so loved
the *world*."

TIME-ENDURING, NOT TRANSIENT

Moreover, just as the love of God is not limited to any one
nation or class, so it is not limited to any one *time*. When John
iii. 16 says: "God so loved the *world*," it includes not only the
nineteen hundred millions now scattered throughout the five
continents, but all the other hundreds of millions in every generation from Adam downwards, and all the hundreds of millions
yet to be born. The great declaration of our text not only looks
northward and southward and eastward and westward; it looks
backward and forward. All the millions who lived in the era
B.C. were included, by anticipation, in the redeeming sacrifice
of Calvary; for God loved, and still loves *them*, as He loves and
will always love *us*. Well may we sing of this love—

> Immortal love, for ever full,
> Forever flowing free,
> Forever shared, forever whole,—
> A never ebbing sea.

WORLD-WIDE, NOT LOCAL

Truly, John iii. 16 marks a *climax* in the revelation of God's
love to men. When young Jacob fled from his father's tents,
long ago, and lay down for the night, with the open country
everywhere around him, and the great dark sky everywhere
above him, he fell asleep with a strange sense of littleness and
loneliness in his mind, but he awoke from his dream, exclaiming,
"Surely the Lord is in this place, and I knew it not!" Jacob
had assumed that his father's God was now left miles behind,
in his father's tents. It had never occurred to him that this
God could be elsewhere. But now he exclaims: "Surely the
Lord is in *this* place!"—and later he was to discover that his
father's God was with him in *every* place.

Hundreds of years later, when the Syrians fought against Israel, they sought to join battle with Israel on some lowland plain, because, as they thought, Israel's God was only a god of the hills. This childish conception of localised deities was everywhere prevalent at that time, and, alas, survives even to-day in parts of the earth where Christianity has not dispersed such superstitions. Within Israel, however, the educative process steadily won through, whereby the nation came to believe and also to teach other nations the universality of the one true God.

David himself had come to know God thus, as we see in Psalm cxxxix—"If I ascend up into heaven, Thou art there; if I make my bed in Sheol, behold, Thou art there! If I take the wings of the morning (the utmost east), or dwell in the uttermost parts of the sea (the utmost west), even there shall Thy hand lead me, and Thy right hand shall hold me. If I say: Surely the darkness shall cover me; even the night shall be light about me. Yea, the darkness hideth not from Thee; but the night shineth as the day: the darkness and the light are both alike to Thee."

Solomon, also, is awake to the same awe-inspiring truth. Hear his noble words at the dedication of the Temple—"Lord God of Israel, there is no God like Thee, in heaven above or on earth beneath . . . Behold the heaven and heaven of heavens cannot contain Thee, how much less this house that I have builded?" And even though a circumscribed prophet like Jonah could foolishly seek to escape from Jehovah's presence by taking ship to Tarshish, yet with such kings as David and Solomon, and such prophets as Isaiah and Jeremiah, Israel came eventually to a true conception of God, as "The everlasting God, the Lord, the Creator of the ends of the earth."

Moreover, this process gradually forced a recognition of the fact, not only that "all kindreds of the earth" were Jehovah's, but that He had beneficent interests in, and purposes for, the nations other than Israel. The crowning point was reached when the incarnate Son of God Himself uttered the never-to-be-forgotten words to Nicodemus: "For *God so loved the world*, that He gave His only begotten Son, that whosoever believeth in Him should not perish, but have everlasting life."

INDIVIDUAL, NOT MERELY COLLECTIVE

But we must never think that God loves us only in a collective way, or *en masse*. His love is as individualistic as it is all-inclusive. He loves us not merely as a species, but as individual souls. That God can love the whole human race, with all its millions, in all five continents, both past and present, and single out each member of such a vast family, seems impossible to these little minds of ours. Yet this is how God loves. Nor does He *divide* His love among us. He loves each of us with the whole of His love. We can best illustrate this—though only feebly at best— by a mother's love for her children. You know how a mother lavishes her love on her first little one. There never was a babe quite so sweet as this one; and her whole heart goes out to it. Well, what happens to that mother's love for this little one when other young lives are born into the family? Does the mother divide her love into four parts, and devote a fourth part to each of her four children? Of course not. Even to ask such a question sounds absurd. She loves each child with the whole of her love. This is the glory of a mother's love: and this is how God loves us. He loves *all* of us—and *each* of us. Let each grateful heart say it softly—God loves *me*. Yes, God so loved *me*, that He gave His only begotten Son to die for *me*, and to save *me*.

Oh, what wealth of precious comfort is in these words! Surely this is the deepest inspiration of all overseas missionary enter-prise—that God loves every man, woman, and child on earth, that Jesus died for every one of us, whatever be our race or colour, and that all men and women and children have a right to hear of this redeeming love. We cannot find one human being on this earth whom God does not love. Each soul is precious to Him; and therefore the Christian missionary goes forth, saying with Paul: "Woe is me if I preach not the Gospel!"

And now, dear friend, can you not believe that this great love of God includes *you*? And can you not understand that it was in His great love for you that "God so loved the world that He gave His only begotten Son, that whosoever believeth in Him should not perish, but have everlasting life"? Have you yet realised that, as a sinner, you are "perishing" if you are without Christ? And will you not by faith accept Jesus, even now, as your Sin-bearer and Saviour? God's word says that whosoever believeth on Him "shall never perish," but "have everlasting life." Oh, this wonderful love of God, this glorious fountainhead of redemption! God grant that we may worthily respond to it, and never cease our praises for it!

> Come let us sing of a wonderful love,
>   Tender and true;
> Out of the heart of the Father above,
>   Streaming to me and to you;
> Wonderful love, wonderful love
> Dwells in the heart of the Father above.

THAT WORD "PERISH"

The truth of an eternal hell, when really accepted, has a far deeper sanctifying effect than is ever realised. The horror of it, which completely outweighs our fiercest anger, is a horror so unspeakable that our entire attitude is revolutionised. As fellow-sinners saved by grace alone we sink back into utter silence, all anger gone: the wickedest man we have ever known becomes solely an object of pity: *hate dies, and love is born.* This appalling truth is also, naturally and inevitably, *the source of more saved souls* than will ever be known. The words of Dr. Watts record what is the Church's experience of two millenniums: "I never knew but one person in the whole course of my ministry, who acknowledged that the first motions of religion in their heart arose from a sense of the goodness of God, and that they were gently and sweetly led at first to this enquiry, 'What shall I render to the Lord, who hath dealt so bountifully with me?' But I think all besides, who have come within my notice, have rather been first awakened by *the passion of fear,* to fly from the wrath to come."

D. M. Panton

THAT WORD "PERISH"

"Should not perish"—John iii. 16.

A MAN once came to C. H. Spurgeon, with a poser from the Bible. "There now," he said, "can you tell me what *that* means?" With a twinkle in his eye, Spurgeon replied: "Why, of course I can tell you what it means. *It means just what it says.*" Now it is a strange fact that many of us, when we read the great invitations and solemn warnings of God's word, vaguely assent to them without really believing that they mean *just what they say.* As it was with the man in the Gospel narrative, who cried: "Lord, I believe; help Thou mine unbelief," so to-day there is a kind of unbelieving believing; and it is very common. Many persons will tell us that they believe in Jesus; and yet they obviously do not trust or obey or love or serve Him, or in any way relate their life to Him. Many persons will tell us they believe that Jesus died on the Cross to be our Saviour; yet they have never received Jesus as their own personal Saviour, nor does it appear ever to have occurred to them that they needed to do so. Many persons will readily affirm that Jesus rose from the grave; yet they live as though He were dead. Many persons will admit belief in a coming Judgment Day; yet they live as though they were utterly unaccountable to a holy God. This unbelieving believing is strangely paradoxical, but it is common enough. It is a kind of believing merely with the upper part of the mind which leaves the heart itself undisturbed. If it were a *real* believing it would stir the heart and move the will and change the life.

How many people there are who readily believe the words of our text and yet do not believe them at all! Yet never were more tremendous words written than these—"That whosoever believeth in Him should not *perish,* but have everlasting life."

93

May we ourselves not be guilty of carelessly nodding to them without thoughtfully heeding them! May God's Spirit burn into our hearts the realisation that these solemn and glorious words really mean *just what they say*!

DOES THE WORD REALLY MEAN PERISH?

Yes, these words mean just what they say; and they tell us the *purpose* which lies behind all God's loving and giving as revealed in the Gospel, namely, that we might be *eternally saved*. There is no getting over that ugly word "perish." It is actually in the text; and it means just what it says—"that whosoever believeth in Him should not *perish*." It may be asked if that word "perish" is a true translation here. Does the Greek word so translated really mean "perish"? The answer is that our English word "perish" is not even a shade too harsh to represent the Greek word here. If we wish to verify this we can easily turn to other verses where this Greek word occurs. For instance, it comes in Matthew v. 29, where we have our Lord's solemn words: "If thy right eye offend thee, pluck it out and cast it from thee, for it is profitable for thee that one of thy members should *perish*, and not that thy whole body should be cast into hell." It comes again in Matthew viii. 25, where we find the almost shipwrecked disciples exclaiming: "Lord, save us; we *perish*!" And again it turns up in chapter ix. 17, where Jesus, speaking of the old-time skin bottles, says: "Neither do men put new wine into old bottles, else the bottles break, and the wine runneth out, and the bottles *perish*." Sometimes this Greek word is translated by our word "destroy." It is thus rendered in Matthew ii. 13: "Arise, and take the young child and his mother, and flee into Egypt, and be thou there until I bring thee word; for Herod will seek the young child to *destroy* him." Here, then, are a few occurrences of this Greek word, chosen almost at random from the first book of the New Testament. As an example of its use elsewhere in the New Testament, take 1 Corinthians x. 9, 10, where our English word "destroyed" is again used to translate it: "Neither let us tempt Christ, as some of them (the old-time Israelites) tempted, and were *destroyed* of serpents. Neither murmur ye, as some of them also murmured, and were *destroyed* of the destroyer."

There can be no doubt, then, that this word in John iii. 16 really means "perish." The plucked-out eye perishes. The sailor, if he is drowned, perishes. The burst skin-bottle perishes. The young child, if murdered, perishes. The serpent-bitten Israelites perished.

THE WORD AS USED OF THE SOUL

Yes, all these instances are quite clear, but the awful thing is that in John iii. 16 this word "perish" is used in a *spiritual* sense. In all the passages just cited the word is used in a physical sense only. The plucked-out eye and the burst skin-bottle are physical things, and the perishing is a physical perishing. When the word is used of the sailor drowned in the deep, or of the infant slain by the sword, it means the death of the body, a perishing physically. The serpent-bitten Israelites who died long ago perished physically, inasmuch as their carcases fell in the wilderness. But here, in John iii. 16, the word is used of the *soul*. There is always the underlying thought of tragedy even when we speak merely about the perishing of the body; but what a depthless tragedy must the perishing of a *soul* be! When the body perishes it gradually decomposes; so that besides having lost all *consciousness*, it loses any separate *existence*: but the soul does not perish with, or like, the body: it does not lose either its existence or its individual consciousness. Nothing is more plainly taught in Scripture than that. What, then, can this word "perish" mean, as used of the soul? It must mean something awful; for, as the word "perish" is used to denote the extreme evil which can overtake the body, so, in being now used of the soul, it is obviously meant to denote the extreme evil which can befall the soul.

THE WORD IN ITS DREAD MEANING

As used of physical things, the word "perish" always carries the thought of *destruction*. The plucked-out eye is destroyed. The burst bottle is destroyed. The drowned sailor and the infant slain by the sword are destroyed. The serpent-bitten Hebrews, whose carcases perished in the wilderness, are destroyed. That thought of destruction is always present in the word "perish," when used of things physical. So is it when the word is used of the soul; though here, of course, since the soul is non-physical, it does not imply destruction in the sense of extinction, or cessation of consciousness. It signifies a final *condition* of the soul. It means the destruction of all those qualities within the soul which constitute its true life and well-being, with the consequent expulsion of the soul, in the eternal Beyond, from that environment in which alone it can know joy. Sin entered the human race through our first parents, and has prevailed within the race ever since, distancing man from God, in a spiritual sense, so that now—to quote the words of Scripture—by their hereditary nature, men are "alienated from the life of God, through the ignorance that is in them"; and it is this state of alienation from God which makes the soul the prey of those evil dispositions which, unless expurgated by regeneration, ultimately sink it into the abysmal ruin indicated in this word "perish."

DAMNATION BY JUDICIAL SENTENCE

We are not just giving the rein to morbid imagination when we speak of souls being "lost" in the hereafter. There is no mistaking the warnings of God's word. Moreover, it is well to realise that the Scriptures attribute this final tragedy of the soul to two factors—to a judicial *sentence* passed upon the soul by the Divine Judge, and to a *process* operating within the soul itself. Mark that fact well: eternal death is both a penalty and an issue. The one is the legal aspect; the other is the moral aspect. The one refers to sins (acts) committed; the other refers to sin (a state) contracted. Sins (plural) mean *guilt*, and call for judgment. Sin (singular) is *disease*, and brings its own hell of torment.

Plainly enough do the Scriptures pre-announce a final judgment at which sentence will be passed on souls. Equally plainly do they teach that the basis of this judgment will be "the *deeds* done in the body," and that the sentence will be "according to their *works*." Twice over, in his description of the coming judgment, John says: "They were judged . . . according to their *works*" (Rev. xx. 12, 13). This is as one would expect, for sentence is always passed on what a man has *done*, not upon what he *is*. In other words, sentence has to do with transgression, not with condition. Let us keep this clearly in mind, then, that the destiny of souls is, in one aspect, the outcome of a sentence which is passed and a penalty which is imposed. That awful reality which the Scriptures call "the lake of fire" and "the second death," is said to be a *penalty* for sin. It is not the only penalty; but it is the *extreme* penalty. Well may we cry in the ears of impenitent sinners: "It is a fearful thing to fall into the hands of the living God!"

DAMNATION BY SPIRITUAL PROCESS

But there is that other aspect, equally real and awful, namely, that souls are lost through a *process* operating within the soul itself. In other words, that final tragedy of the soul, in the Beyond, is the culmination of that which goes on in the soul in this present life on earth. There are those who go on in ways of sin fondly dreaming that somehow, in the end, they will elude the sentence of the dread judge. They certainly never will elude that "great white throne" before which mankind will be arraigned; but even if they *could*, would that spare them from torment? Not at all: for their hell will be kindled by what they *are* in themselves, by the natural and inevitable culmination of their progressive sinning. We are so constituted, as human beings, that we simply cannot sin without suffering. Our condition in the *next* life is inseparable from our character in *this* life. In the fields of eternal destiny we reap as we have sown. If I read my Bible rightly, heaven and hell are real places: but the fact to grasp just here is that what makes heaven or hell in the after-sphere is not so much *where* we are as *what* we are. It has been often and truly said that "heaven is a prepared place for a prepared people." Heaven begins in the *heart*, down here, before it is consummated in the *home*, up there. And what is true of heaven, in this sense, is true of hell. Many a man's hell will be *himself*. The flames of Gehenna will be but the final, inescapable, quenchless burnings of those pampered passions and lusts which have been allowed to inflame the soul in this present life; so that even if a man might possibly escape sentence from his Divine Judge, he simply cannot escape from *himself*.

AN INESCAPABLE CULMINATION

How awful, then, is it to live in ways of sin during this present life on earth! There is no escape. "God is not mocked: whatsoever a man soweth, that shall he also reap." Foolishly enough, men and women have imagined that if death did not end all for them, then at any rate they would start all over anew in the other realm. One of the greatest purposes of the New Testament is to warn us against such a foolish misconception, and to open our eyes wide to this fact that we cannot possibly escape the outworking of the process which goes on in the soul in this present life and is culminated in the eternal Beyond.

Away in a tropical country, a traveller was attacked by a snake. He fled from it, but it pursued him. Almost breathless he came to a river and plunged through to the other side, so that the flowing water might mercifully separate him from his danger. But scarcely had he reached the farther bank before he heard the hiss of the reptile behind him, and on looking round saw to his horror that it had followed him through the river—it was a water snake! Even so do men's sins follow them through the river of death, and find them out in the life beyond. Moses never spoke a truer word than when he said: "Be sure your sin will find you out." Some men's sins find them out, and exact their sorry toll, even in this present life. Those who have lived impurely or inebriately are often "found out" by loathsome disease of the body. Those other kinds of sinning which do not scourge us with such outward, physical retribution, find us out, none the less in our minds. No man can ever secretly indulge evil thoughts without finding that eventually his whole mind becomes a cage of unclean birds, a den of toads and reptiles, a malarial swamp, an internal hell, from which he screams to escape but without avail.

All sin finds us out in some way, because of that process which is ever going on in human souls, just as all holy aspirings and heavenward strivings bring their certain reward. We cannot extricate ourselves from this process; and even those sins which do not find us out in this present life cross the dark river with us, and sting the soul with their burning venom in the life beyond. Death may bring about a separation of soul and body, but it cannot dissolve the soul itself, or separate a man from what he is in himself. As the tree falls, so it lies; and as a man dies, so he goes into eternity. The drunkard takes his mad craving, and the glutton his inflamed appetites. The miser takes his frenzied greed, and the man enslaved to foul habits takes his deadly chains. The sensual man takes his insatiate passions, and the man of violent hate his maddening tempers. These cravings and passions will create a hell of their own, quite apart from any sentence passed by the divine Judge; for they will rage like a fever, without there being any possibility of gratification. Surely this is "the worm that dieth not" and "the fire that is not quenched." If the rich man lifted up his eyes in Hades, "being in torments" (Luke xvi. 23), what must it be to become engulfed in that "lake of fire" which is Gehenna! Oh, what woeful depth of meaning there is in that word "perish"! We would urge every soul without Christ to pause and reflect on these words of our text—"that whosoever believeth in Him should not *perish*. . . ."

A PRESENT PROCESS

We have already pointed out that the word "perish" here points to that final condition of ruin which is the *culmination* of a present process; but it is well to stress the fact that inasmuch as this process is even now operating in this present life, those souls which are closed against Christ are *even now perishing*. That this is so is clearly taught in the pages of the New Testament. Take the following verses, which I will read from the Revised Version. In 1 Corinthians i. 18, Paul says: "The word of the Cross is foolishness to *them that are perishing*." In 2 Corinthians iv. 3, we read: "If our gospel is veiled, it is veiled in *them that are perishing*." Again, in 2 Thessalonians ii. 10, we are told that the antichrist shall deceive "*them that are perishing*" because they have "received not the love of the truth, that they might be saved."

Incidentally, such verses as these are a sure *test* by which we may know whether we ourselves are among the perishing or not. Take the first of them—"The word of the Cross is foolishness to them that are perishing." Is the Cross of Jesus, as the one way of salvation, something which I treat with superior scorn?—then I am perishing. Those who know the power of that Cross to justify the repentant and believing sinner, glory in it. If I disdain the Cross, then that is proof enough that I am not saved by it, and that I am perishing in my unbelief. Take the next verse—"If our gospel is veiled, it is veiled in them that are perishing." Is the warm and shining message of God's redeeming love something which leaves me coldly unmoved? Is Christ merely as "a root out of a dry ground," having "no form nor comeliness" that I should desire Him? Then I am perishing; for Satan has cast his dark veil over my heart lest I should see the light of the Gospel and the beauty of Christ. This, indeed, is what the verse says— "If our gospel is veiled, it is veiled in them that are perishing; in whom the god of this world hath blinded the minds of the unbelieving, that the light of the gospel of the glory of Christ, who is the image of God, should not dawn upon them." Yes, if the Gospel is veiled to me, I am perishing.

Take the third verse, which speaks of the antichrist deceiving "them that are perishing" because they have "received not the love of the truth, that they might be saved." Am I knowingly refusing to receive "the truth as it is in Christ Jesus"?—then I am perishing; for this is the only truth that regenerates the soul. Did I once have "the love of the truth," so that I was glad to hear the Gospel, whereas now, through prolonged procrastination to receive the Saviour, my heart has grown impervious, so that I have lost even "the *love* of the truth"?—then I am certainly perishing.

Oh, my friends, it is an awful thing to perish! We would urge every Christless soul: Be wise to escape that eternal damnation which is called "the lake of fire" and "the second death." Make haste to the hill called Calvary. See there the only begotten Son of God making atonement for all our sin. Look to Him by faith and be saved. Open the heart to His incoming; for He who hung there long ago now knocks at the heart's door. He is no longer on the Cross, for His atonement is a completed work. He is no longer in the grave, for death is a conquered foe. None need perish, for God now offers pardon and a full salvation to all who turn from their sins and accept the Saviour. Come now to the good Shepherd who gave His life for the sheep; for He says of all His sheep:—"I give unto them eternal life, and they shall *never perish.*" Oh, look to Him now. Give ear to this wonderful Gospel which calls to us down the years—"God so loved the world that He gave His only begotten Son, that whosoever believeth in Him *should not perish*, but have everlasting life."

ETERNAL LIFE

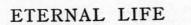

Oh, Christ, He is the fountain,
　The deep, sweet well of love!
The streams on earth I've tasted,
　More deep I'll drink above.
There, to an ocean fulness,
　His mercy doth expand,
And glory—*glory* dwelleth
　In Immanuel's land.

Soon shall the cup of glory
　Wash down earth's bitter woes,
Soon shall the desert-briar
　Break into Eden's rose!
Oh, to join Hallelujah
　With yon triumphant band,
Who sing, where glory dwelleth,
　In Immanuel's land!

Mrs. A. R. Cousin

ETERNAL LIFE

"But have everlasting life"—John iii. 16.

THE TWO words, "perish" and "life," here stand in sheer contrast. They represent the two ultimate extremes of human destiny. The one word plunges our thought down to the deepest conceivable depth of ruin: the other wings our thought upward to the highest conceivable height of felicity. We have already considered something of the tragic meaning contained in the word "perish". Let us now turn our minds to that which is here set forth as the glorious alternative, namely, "everlasting life." First of all, however, in place of the word "everlasting" let us read "eternal," as in more recent versions. It is unfortunate that our Authorised Version should have used the word "everlasting" here, when in the verse just before this one it translates the same Greek word as "eternal." What then is "eternal life"?

NOT MERE ENDLESSNESS

To begin with, this expression, "eternal life," does not mean merely an *endless duration*. That is why, in preferring the word "eternal" to "everlasting," in this verse, we are not just hair-splitting, but are making a distinction of real importance. That which is everlasting is simply without end: but that which is eternal is without either end or beginning. We shall touch on this again shortly. The word "everlasting," we say, suggests simply endless duration; whereas the expression "eternal life" is meant to convey the thought, not just of bare duration, but of quality. It has a qualitative as well as a quantitative import. Certainly, the idea of unlimited continuity is prominently present in the expression, as many of its occurrences in the New Testament clearly show: but there is the equally vital conception of supreme quality also present, as other New Testament references imply. When Paul says: "The things which are seen are temporal; but the things which are not seen are eternal," it is quite clear that the word "eternal" is meant to express *unendingness*, in antithesis to the word "temporal." But when the Lord Jesus says to the Father: "This is life eternal, that they might know Thee, the only true God," the thought of a supreme quality of life is evidently present. It is this union of the words "eternal" and "life" which transforms the sterile concept of mere unendingness into one of aeonian fulness and glory. Let us clearly grasp this then, that "eternal life" is not just endless duration.

THE IMPARTED LIFE OF GOD

Interpreted in the light of other New Testament passages, the expression "eternal life" here means the very life of God Himself, as revealed in a unique way to men in Jesus Christ, and actually *imparted*, through Him, to all who by faith become savingly united to Him. There is a real sense, of course, in which the life of God is revealed through everything He has created. The universe reveals His power and wisdom; and all that has emanated from His creative will may be said to express Him. But in Jesus Christ there is the unique revelation of the *moral qualities* of the divine life; and this unique revelation is only possible because Christ, the Only begotten, is Himself Divine, eternally one with the Father, eternally expressing the Father, and now, in time, the incarnate embodiment of the Divine life, before men. The revelation is not simply *through* Him; but *in* Him; for He is not simply a medium, but the Life itself. Thus we find John saying: "The Life was manifested, and we have seen, and bear witness, and show unto you that *Eternal Life* which was with the Father, and was manifested unto us" (1 John i. 2).

Christ, then, is the very embodiment of the Divine life. He is, indeed, in Himself, the eternal life of God manifested to men. And the sequence to this is found in these further words of John: "God hath given *us* eternal life, and this life is *in* His Son. *He that hath the Son hath the life*" (1 John v. 11, 12). This truth, that the eternal life of the Godhead is first *expressed* to us in

Christ, and then *imparted* to us through Him, is found again and again in the New Testament. In John i. 14–16, we read: "The Word was made flesh, and dwelt among us. . . . And of His fulness have all *we* received." Paul writes: "In Him dwelleth all the fulness of the Godhead bodily: and *ye* are filled full in Him" (Col. ii. 9, 10). But the most clear-cut pronouncement is that by John, which we have already quoted: "God hath given us eternal life, and this life is in His Son. *He that hath the Son hath the life.*" The impartation of this eternal life to the Christian believer does not make the believer himself divine. The believer remains an individual human personality; but there is imparted to him, from God and through Christ, that true life containing within itself all those moral qualities which together constitute unending blessedness.

A PRESENT POSSESSION

This eternal life is *a present possession* of the Christian believer. In John iii. 36 we read: "He that believeth on the Son *hath* eternal life." The Lord Jesus Himself says, in John v. 24: "He that heareth My word, and believeth on Him that sent Me, *hath* eternal life." Again, in His great discourse on the bread of life, He says: "He that believeth on Me *hath* eternal life" (John vi. 47). Paul tells us that "the gift of God *is*—here and now—eternal life, through (or in) Jesus Christ our Lord" (Rom. vi. 23); and in many other ways Paul speaks of this life as being the Christian's present possession,—in such phrases and clauses, for instance, as "Christ *in you*," "Christ, our *life*," "Christ liveth *in me*," "The Spirit of life . . . dwelleth *in you*." And, as though to settle the matter conclusively, John writes, at the end of his epistle: "These things have I written unto you that believe on the name of the Son of God, that ye may KNOW that ye HAVE eternal life." This is a glorious truth, and a thrilling reality to those who walk in close communion with the risen Lord. The sad thing is that although this truth is thus clearly taught in the New Testament, the eyes of very many others—preachers and hearers alike—seem closed to it. This message of eternal life as a present possession is the greatest that the Christian pulpit can declare. Men will not be won by the inculcating of bare religious principles: the need is *life*; and this life is offered here and now in Jesus Christ.

THE BELIEVER'S INHERITANCE

Again, because this life is "eternal" and not merely "ever-lasting," it becomes, in a wonderful way, the believer's *inheritance*. It is not only something which is possessed from now onwards: it is an eternal wealth into which the saved believer enters as a participant. We begin to see here why the word of God says that the believer has "*eternal*," not merely "everlasting," life. Dr. A. T. Pierson explains as follows. "Suppose you are born of a certain noble sire and mother, and trace your lineage back, through all the generations to a remote antiquity; you, as a child of the family, are not only entitled to all that pertains to that family in the future, but you inherit all that pertains to that family in the past. The glory of its past history, of its achievements, of its heroism on the battlefield, of its services in the state or church; the glory of its learning, of its patriotism, of its philanthropy,— you, as a child in that family, come into the inheritance of it all. Even so there is a spiritual heredity. If I am a child of God by faith in Jesus Christ, all the past of God I inherit as well as all the future of God. Being a child of God, whatever is glorious in the past eternity of God comes to enrich my present and my future. When God has a child born to Him in His family by faith in Jesus Christ, the child does not simply start with the present moment of birth to enjoy a future that shall be blessed; but God enriches that new heir of glory by all that there is in the glorious past of His eternal existence. You have God for your Father, and all God's past is, in Christ, your past also."

A FUTURE CONSUMMATION

Still further, this "eternal life," although even now in the possession of the believer, has reference to a *future consummation*. Just as there are verses in the New Testament which unmistakably denote that the expression "eternal life" means a quality of life now imparted to the believer, so there are other verses which equally definitely show that the expression has special reference to futurity. For instance, our Lord says: "He that loveth his life shall lose it; and he that hateth his life in this world shall keep

it unto life eternal" (John xii. 25). Here the thought is evidently
upon that life which is beyond the present. Similarly, when the
apostle Paul speaks of "the *hope* of eternal life" (Titus i. 2), he is
thinking of a consummation away in the future. So is John,
when he writes: "This is the *promise* that He hath promised us,
even eternal life" (1 John ii. 25). There are other verses along
the same line, but we need not quote them here. They all use this
expression "eternal life" to point onwards to a glorious consummation yet to be. They do not rule out those other passages in
which "eternal life" signifies a life already imparted to the believer, but they do teach us that our entering into the *full realisation*
of that eternal glory which is summed up in the expression "eternal life," is yet future. What that coming glory will be, who can
describe? Neither our physical senses nor our faculty of imagination can give us any adequate conception of it. It will be life in
its fullest, richest, purest, sweetest, and most glorious quality.

RESURRECTION AND IMMORTALITY

In this future sense, "eternal life" includes *immortality*. Now
this word "immortality" is often used of the soul; but strictly
speaking it refers only to the *body*. In 2 Timothy i. 10, Paul tells
us that the Lord Jesus "hath abolished death, and hath brought
life and immortality to light through the gospel." Note the two
words, "life" and "immortality." They are not just two words
for the same thing. The word "life" refers to the soul, and the
word "immortality" to the body. This word "immortality"
comes again in 1 Corinthians xv. 53, where Paul is speaking of
the resurrection of the body: "For this corruptible must put on
incorruption, and this mortal must put on immortality." Immortality, then, refers to the *body*. There is, therefore, only One
in all the universe who has immortality, and that is "the Man
Christ Jesus." This is because "Christ being raised from the dead
dieth no more: death hath no more dominion over Him." It is
not just that the spirit of Jesus passed into the presence of God:
He was raised *bodily* from among the dead. He was seen again,
in the *body*. He ascended to heaven with that resurrection *body*.
He is the pledge of the coming resurrection and immortality of the

bodies of all His blood-sealed people; but at present He alone has immortality; and, therefore, Paul speaks of Him, in 1 Timothy vi. 16, as "the King of kings and Lord of lords, *who only hath immortality*." Oh what rapturous consummation it will be when we enter into the full meaning of that expression "eternal life," and at the same time find that the glorious fulness of being which has become ours is able to express itself with perfect felicity through bodies that have become glorified and immortalised!

> Then we will be what we would be;
> And we shall be what we should be;
> Things that are not now, nor could be,
> Then shall be our own!

Again and again we find this thought of the resurrection and immortality of the body going with the thought of eternal life. Turn back to the Lord's discourse on the bread of life. He says: "This is the will of Him that sent Me, that every one which seeth the Son, and believeth on Him, may have eternal life; *and I will raise him up at the last day*." Four times over in this discourse does the Saviour use these words, pledging the bodily resurrection of all who have received the eternal life which He came to impart; and the words are spoken in such a way as to indicate that this promised immortality of the body is the complement of the "eternal life." This hope of the resurrection of the body to immortal life thenceforward becomes the great hope of those who have found the "eternal life" in Christ, as we see in such passages as Romans viii. 23, and Philippians iii. 20: "Ourselves also, which have the firstfruits of the Spirit (the indwelling life), groan within ourselves, waiting for the adoption, the redemption of the body." "Our citizenship is in heaven, from whence, also, we look for the Saviour the Lord Jesus Christ; who shall change our body of humiliation, that it may be fashioned like unto His own body of glory." What a hope this is! No wonder that John, having said: "We shall be *like Him*, for we shall see Him as He is," adds— "And every man that hath this hope set upon Him purifieth himself."

THE RICHES OF ETERNAL GLORY

Finally, this "eternal life," in its futuristic sense, comprises in one, all those many glorious *rewards and blessings in the hereafter* which the word of God pledges to the Christian believer. The New Testament well nigh exhausts figures of speech in trying to give us some little conception of that rapturous life, that pure bliss, that endless blessedness, which is the portion of the redeemed throughout the ages to come. In one place it is called "an exceeding and eternal weight of glory" (2 Cor. iv. 17). In another place it is called a being "glorified together (with Christ)" (Rom. viii. 17). In another place it is called a "glorious liberty of the sons of God" (Rom. viii. 21). In another place it is called "an inheritance, incorruptible, and undefiled, and that fadeth not away, reserved in heaven" (1 Pet. i. 4). It is a swallowing up of death in victory (1 Cor. xv. 54). It is a being "changed from glory to glory" (2 Cor. iii. 18). It is a seeing "face to face," and a knowing "even as we are known" (1 Cor. xiii. 12). It is "the prize of the high calling of God in Christ Jesus" (Phil. iii. 14). It is "the inheritance of the saints in light" (Col. i. 12). It is a being "ever with the Lord" (1 Thess. iv. 17). It is a dwelling in "mansions" prepared for us in "the Father's house" (John xiv. 2). It is a "reigning together" with Christ (2 Tim. ii. 12). It is the servant's entering into the joy of his Lord (Matt. xxv. 21). It is the enjoying of "a better country, that is, a heavenly" (Heb. xi. 16). It is a being "presented faultless before the presence of His glory with exceeding joy" (Jude 24). It is the enjoyment of the "exceeding riches of His grace" throughout "the ages to come" (Eph. ii. 7). It is all these things and many more, so that language breaks down, and Paul can only say: "Eye hath not seen, nor ear heard, neither have entered into the heart of man, the things which God hath prepared for them that love Him" (1 Cor. ii. 9); and John has to say: "Beloved . . . it doth not yet appear what we shall be." Whatever all these delectable prospects mean, who shall say, or who can even imagine? But they are all included in "eternal life"!

THE FINAL PICTURE

Turn to the last chapter of the Bible, and see God's own picture of that final glory.

"There shall be no more curse; but the throne of God and of the Lamb shall be in it; and His servants shall serve Him; and they shall see His face; and His name shall be in their foreheads. And there shall be no night there; and they need no candle, neither light of the sun; for the Lord God giveth them light; and they shall reign for ever and ever" (Rev. xxii. 3–5).

See the seven-fold perfection here: perfect *sinlessness*—"no more curse"; perfect *government*—"the throne of God and the Lamb"; perfect *service*—"His servants shall (thus) serve Him"; perfect *vision*—"they shall see His face"; perfect *likeness* to Him—"His name shall be in their foreheads"; perfect *enlightenment*—"there shall be no night . . . the Lord God giveth them light"; perfect *glory*—"they shall reign for ever and ever." Such is the peerless consummation of "eternal life" in the ages to come!

What, then, shall we say to these things? Two facts stand out in clear relief. First, "eternal life" may be said to be the sum of all that blessedness, both here and hereafter, which becomes the Christian believer's through union with Christ. Second, "eternal life" is the diametric opposite of that which is meant by the word "perish." The two terms stand in infinite contrast, representing two eternal realities. Thank God, there is a Gospel which tells of a Saviour who died for sinners, so that "whosoever believeth in Him should not perish, but have eternal life!" O soul without Christ, mark well these alternatives— "perish" and "eternal life." God grant that through faith in the Saviour we may escape the one and possess the other!

WHAT IS SAVING FAITH?

It does not depend on any power or merit in man; no, not in any degree, neither in whole, nor in part. It does not in any wise depend either on the good works, or righteousness of the receiver; not on anything he has done, or anything he is. It does not depend on his endeavours. It does not depend on his good tempers, or good desires, or good purposes and intentions. For all these flow from the free grace of God; they are the streams only, not the fountain. They are the fruits of free grace, and not the root. They are not the cause, but the effects of it. Thus is His grace free in all, that is, no way depending on any power or merit in man; but on God alone, who freely gave us His own Son, and "with Him freely giveth us all things."

John Wesley

WHAT IS SAVING FAITH?

"That whosoever believeth . . ."—John iii. 16.

SOME years ago I attended a debate between a so-called free-thinker and a Presbyterian minister. The free-thinker's case against Christianity was pathetically sincere and boyishly superficial. The Presbyterian minister had an easy task to reply, and a fine opportunity of explaining the Gospel to a crowd of free-thinkers at the same time as he answered their spokesman; but he failed, and failed badly, by displaying a superior knowledge of Aristotle and Plato instead of sticking to his Bible.

The free-thinker's case was this: Christianity lays down certain propositions, and then says that if you believe them you will be eternally saved, but that if you do not believe them you will be eternally damned. He turned us to three texts to prove this. The first was Mark xvi. 16: "He that believeth and is baptised shall be saved; but he that believeth not shall be damned." The second was John iii. 36: "He that believeth on the Son hath everlasting life; and he that believeth not the Son shall not see life, but the wrath of God abideth on him." The third text I cannot remember for certain, but it was one along the same line. Such an idea, he said, was absurd.

Now the answer to him is simple and obvious. The poor fellow was childishly wrong about that word "believeth." He was miles away from understanding what the New Testament means by believing. In such texts as those which he quoted, the word "believeth" does not mean merely a mental assent to certain propositions. It refers to an act and an attitude of the heart, which moves the will and affects the whole man. That act of the heart which the New Testament calls believing may be quite a *simple* act, in the sense that it is free from any intellectual complicatedness; yet in a moral and spiritual sense, it goes as deep as human nature itself.

There is no doubt about this—the word of God *does* say that salvation comes to us through our "believing"; and since this is so, it is unspeakably important that we should understand as clearly as possible what "faith" or "believing" really is.

WHAT IS SAVING FAITH?

Who shall adequately define faith? Considered in its psychological aspects, it is just about as complicated a subject as one could hit on. This, however, need not deter us in the least just here, for we are not concerned with faith from the standpoint of psychology. We are not at all concerned with the analysing or describing of those intricate mental processes which lie behind it and run through it. After all, what faith *is* can only be really known by what it *does*. Its *nature* is known by the way it *expresses* itself. We all have a general idea of what faith is; and our purpose just here is to make clear that kind of faith which the New Testament says is necessary to the salvation of our souls.

And first, we must clear the ground by answering negatively that the faith which saves the soul is no mere *unreasoning assumption* such as often passes for Christian faith. Sunday after Sunday, both in Protestant and Roman Catholic places of worship, thousands of people keep chanting the words: "I believe," who no more really know what it is to believe, to the saving of their souls, than a worm knows what it is to fly. They could not give any coherent account either of what they believe or why they believe it. Yet these people pass as Christians, and actually think within themselves that they are Christians. Their so-called believing is simply the unreasoning assumption of certain truths which they vaguely take for granted, and in which they have been brought up from their infancy. I have heard tell that George Whitefield once asked a man of this sort: "What do you believe?"; and the man replied: "I believe what the Church believes." So Whitefield asked further: "And what does the Church believe?"; to which the man replied: "Oh, the Church believes what I believe." Whereupon Whitefield again asked:

"What then do you both believe?" and the man replied: "The same as each other." This is about as intelligent as much that passes for Christian faith to-day. It is not really Christian faith at all, but a dreamy credulity which neither saves the soul nor vitally affects the character.

NOT MERE MENTAL ASSENT

And again, as already mentioned, saving faith is not just a *mental assent* to certain propositions. This is where the free-thinker went wrong. This kind of believing is predicated even of the demons, for in James ii. 19 we read: "The devils also believe, and tremble." We may believe that Jesus lived and died and rose again, as the Gospel says He did, and yet never believe with that kind of believing which saves the soul. Admittedly there must be a certain degree of knowledge before we can believe; yet saving faith is not, as many suppose, a *complicated* intellectual achievement, which is only possible through intricate reasoning, and to those who have the time to give to such reasoning. There is nothing mysterious or intellectually involved about a true faith. It is simplicity itself. Indeed, it is so simple that thousands stumble over the very simplicity of it. Lots of people have the strange idea that faith is something which can only be attained by theologians or highbrow thinkers. But this is a pathetic misconception. There is nothing abstruse or complicated in that faith which God has appointed as the way of salvation. That is why the New Testament represents it as something within the reach of the lowest and feeblest sinner, and within the comprehension of the most ignorant and uneducated.

FAITH TOWARD A PERSON

What then—to answer now in a positive way—is this faith which the New Testament says is necessary to the salvation of the soul? Well, it clears a whole lot of misunderstanding away when we realise that this faith, or believing, is exercised *towards a Person*. It is not just a matter of believing certain facts or doctrines, but of believing a Person; and that Person is the Lord

Jesus Christ. Dr. Wilbur Chapman brings this out beautifully in telling of his conversion. When he was a young man at College he heard that D. L. Moody was to preach in Chicago, and went to hear him. He stayed to the after-meeting, and was thrilled when Mr. Moody came and sat down beside him. After asking him a few questions Mr. Moody opened his Bible at John v. 24, where Jesus says: "Verily, verily, I say unto you, He that heareth My word, and believeth on Him that sent Me, *hath* everlasting life, and shall not come into condemnation, but is passed from death unto life." Mr. Moody said: "Suppose you had read that for the first time, wouldn't you think it was wonderful?" He got Wilbur Chapman to read it through, and then asked: "Do you accept it?" Wilbur Chapman said "Yes." So Moody said: "Well, then, are you not a Christian?" To this young Chapman replied: "Mr. Moody, I sometimes think I am, and sometimes I am afraid I am not." Whereupon Moody said: "Read the verse again"; and Chapman did so. Again Moody pressed: "Do you believe it?" and again came the reply: "Yes." And again the further question: "Well, then, are you a Christian?" Wilbur Chapman was just starting to say all over again that sometimes he thought he was and sometimes feared he was not, when Moody turned on him with flashing eyes, and said: "See here, young man, *WHOM* are you doubting?" Then, for the first time, young Chapman saw that he was doubting the Lord Jesus Himself, and the very word of God. I wish that all who profess difficulty about believing would realise the same thing. The two attitudes of believing and disbelieving are really directed towards the Lord Jesus Himself. It is not just a matter of believing or disbelieving certain truths. Our believing is a believing exercised toward Jesus Christ; and our doubting or disbelieving, also, is a doubting or disbelieving of Him.

FAITH IN THE SENSE OF TRUST

Now the faith which is to be exercised towards the Lord Jesus is that kind which we call *trust*. When the New Testament speaks about believing "in" or "on" the Lord Jesus it obviously does not mean simply believing certain particulars about Him. It means to rely upon the Lord Jesus *Himself*, as a real, personal Saviour. When we believe *on* a man, we are doing much more than just believing what he says. On occasion we may believe a notoriously untruthful man because, at the time, we may have reason to believe he is telling the truth for once; but to believe *on* a man is to rest with full confidence upon the man himself, as a wife believes on the man she takes for her husband, or as a son believes on the father whose wise and loving guardianship has never failed him.

This kind of believing is an act of the *heart* rather than of the head. Dr. Torrey puts it thus: "To believe on a man means to put confidence in him as what he claims to be. To believe on a physician means to put confidence in him as a physician, resulting in your placing your case in his hands. To believe in a teacher is to put your confidence in him as a teacher, and accept what he teaches. To believe in a banker means to put your confidence in him as a banker, and put your money in his bank. And to believe on the Lord Jesus means to put your confidence in Him as what He claims to be. It is to put confidence in Him as your *Sinbearer*; as your *Deliverer* from the power of sin; as your Divinely infallible *Teacher*; as your *Master* who has the right to the entire control of your life, as your *Guide*, whom you will follow wherever He leads; and as your Divine *Lord*. The moment you thus put your confidence in Jesus Christ, that moment you are saved." Dr. James Denney fitly emphasises that it is not just the *life* of Jesus which saves us, nor even His *death* on Calvary, but *Jesus Himself*, through His atoning death and resurrection. Jesus says: "Believe on *ME*"; and this kind of believing is that which we call *trusting*. No psychologist need be called to explain to us what trusting is. As human beings we are so constituted that we must constantly exercise trust; and we therefore know both by nature and experience what trusting means. When we really trust the Lord Jesus Himself we are saved; for *He* is the Saviour.

There are so many verses in the New Testament which speak about this believing *on* the Lord Jesus, and they speak in such plain language about it, that no honest reader can fail to see its *indispensability*. It is vain for any man to imagine that he is saved simply because Christ came and lived and died and rose

and intercedes, or to think that he is saved because he belongs
to some church, or is baptised, or receives the Lord's Supper,
or engages in some form of religious service. All is of no avail
to save the soul, apart from trust in Jesus Christ Himself. There
is no substitute for this. We must have a personal dealing with
Christ, and exercise a personal reliance upon Him, and know
Him as our own personal Saviour, or we perish.

THIS FAITH INTELLECTUALLY SIMPLE

It is this kind of believing—this act and attitude of trusting
—to which we refer when we speak about being saved by "*simple
faith.*" This kind of believing *is* simple intellectually, so that the
simplest and least educated are capable of it; yet it goes deep
in a moral and spiritual sense. As Bishop Ryle says: "It is the
combined act of the whole man's head, conscience, heart, and
will. It is often so weak and feeble at first, that he who has it
cannot be persuaded that he has it. And yet, like life in the
new-born infant, his belief may be real, genuine, saving, and
true. The moment that the conscience is convinced of sin, and
the head sees Christ to be the only One who can save, and the
heart and will lay hold on the hand that Christ holds out, that
moment there is saving faith. In that moment a man believes."
So then, if we have been puzzled hitherto about faith, thinking
it to be some intricate affair, let us lay this well to heart, that
this faith which we call trusting is indeed a very simple matter
so far as the intellect is concerned, while yet, because it is an
acceptance of, and a committal to, the Lord Jesus, it goes deep
in a moral and spiritual sense—as deep as our nature itself.

ELEMENTARY KNOWLEDGE PRESUPPOSED

Admittedly such faith presupposes a certain amount of *knowledge* even though that knowledge may be of an elementary sort.
Obviously, if we are going to trust something or someone, we
must at least know enough about that thing or person to enable
us to exercise faith intelligently. Saving faith is made up of
three things—knowledge, belief, and trust. Plainly, knowledge

must come first. In the words of Paul—"How shall they believe in Him of whom they have not heard?" We may not know the deeper truths of the New Testament, but we *must* know the elementary facts which the Gospel declares before we can possibly receive it. We may not know anything about the Christian believer's deeper experiences of fellowship with his Lord; but we *must* know certain great facts about the Lord Jesus before we can place our trust in Him as our Saviour. We must know that as a matter of historical fact He lived on earth, and that He taught and wrought as the Scriptures record. We must know, at any rate, that He declared Himself to be the Son of God; that He declared His death to be a ransom for us sinners; that He rose from the dead, and ascended back to the Father; that His character bears testimony to His claim; that above all, His resurrection substantiates His claims to be the incarnate Son of God, and man's Saviour; and that the Scriptures unite in testifying to Him, and offering Him to us as our Saviour. We need not know *more* than this; but there must be *some* such knowledge before there can be faith in Him at all. And then, following this simple knowledge comes *belief*. Having come to know of certain things, the mind goes on to believe them to be true.

So, through this modicum of knowledge, and belief, the soul comes to accept the facts and truths and promises of the Gospel in the sense of *relying* upon them and thus appropriating the glorious blessings which the Gospel offers—the forgiveness of sins, reconciliation and peace with God, the blotting out of guilt, and the justifying of the pardoned sinner, in God's sight, through the merit of the Redeemer. And this act of relying upon the facts and truths and promises of the Gospel, centres in an act of trust in Jesus Himself, as the living embodiment of all the truths and promises of the Gospel, the Son of God and Saviour of all who trust Him.

WHY THIS FAITH SAVES

And now, my friend, can you not trust this Saviour for your own salvation? Do you still feel somehow that your faith is not just enough? Well, if that be so, take comfort from this, that although the Saviour spoke of "much faith," and "little faith," and "great faith," and "no faith," He never said that the smallest amount of faith was inadequate to save the soul! And why is this? It is because, after all, we are not saved by faith as a thing in itself. Faith saves us because it is faith in *CHRIST, THE SAVIOUR*. After all, faith is but the channel, not the fountain head. It is the *object* of faith which gives faith its saving efficacy. A little faith in Christ is worth far more than a big faith in any other. We must never make a Christ out of our very faith, and look upon faith as being in itself the source of our salvation. True faith does not think about itself. Its eye is on Christ alone. Oh that we may learn this well, and fix our eye firmly and finally on the Saviour Himself!

Oh how this heart of mine longs that all whom I now address may trust this Saviour! What reason we have to trust such an One! What depth of sin and need is ours! And what a complete Saviour He is! Can we not even now trust Him with our souls, and become saved? I hope we have seen, from what I have said, that faith is no blind thing, for it begins with knowledge, even though that knowledge is limited. Nor is faith a merely speculative thing, for it fastens on facts of which it has become sure. Nor is it a vague, risky kind of thing, for it rests upon a proven Saviour. Can you not yet accept the Gospel as "glad tidings" from God to sinful men? Can you not yet believe the testimony of God concerning His Son? Can you not yet believe that Jesus keeps all His promises, and that none of all those who have ever trusted Him has He failed? Can you not even now accept pardon and cleansing and justification and preservation, yea and eternal glory from that pierced hand? Oh trust Him at once; trust Him simply and solely; and be forever saved!

> Oh wherefore seek ye for the cause
> Of all the world's unrest and pain?
>   One act of sin,
>   False joy to win,
> In Eden's garden long ago,
>   Was the sad start
>   Within man's heart
> Of all the world's distress and woe.

Oh wherefore seek ye for the cure
Of all the world's unrest and pain?
   One act of grace
   Toward our race,
On yonder Palestinian hill,
   Salvation wrought,
   And healing brought
For all the world's disease and ill.

Oh wherefore seek I still the cure
For all my own unrest and sin?
   One act of faith,
   God's promise saith,
In Him who all my burden bore,
   Brings me His grace,
   Who took my place;
And I am saved, for evermore!

PART TWO

THE OLD TESTAMENT TYPE

We shall treat that word as our Lord regarded it. What was authoritative to Him will be to us; what was history to Him will be to us; what was God's word to Him will be God's word to us; and I don't think we shall go far wrong.

Principal C. Sydney Carter, D.D.

We search the world for truth; we cull
The good, the pure, the beautiful
From graven stone and written scroll,
From all the flower-fields of the soul;
And, weary seekers of the best
We come back laden from our quest,
To find that all the sages said
Is in the Book our mothers read.

J. G. Whittier

THE DECISIVE IMPRIMATUR

IN THE foregoing studies we have considered various aspects of the profound and precious truth contained in John iii. 16. But there is one little word in that text, the significance of which we have not yet considered. It is the first word of the verse, the conjunction, "for"—"FOR God so loved the world . . ."

That "for" is of utmost importance. It connects John iii. 16 with what precedes it in the paragraph, and has significant bearings which merit our closest attention. It indicates that the statement of John iii. 16 *grows out of* what goes before it. And what is it which goes before? It is a reference away back to the Book of Numbers, to the episode of the uplifted brazen serpent which healed the snake-bitten Israelites long ago, on the way to Canaan. Read again the verses which lead to John iii. 16—

"And as Moses lifted up the serpent in the wilderness, even so must the Son of Man be lifted up; that whosoever believeth in Him should not perish, but have everlasting life."

There are those who think that the immortal words of John iii. 16 were not spoken by our Lord Himself, but are John's *comment* upon our Lord's words to Nicodemus. We ourselves do not incline to that view, though we admit that the passage does not settle the matter conclusively either one way or the other. All are agreed, however, that the words about the brazen serpent, in verses 14 and 15, were definitely a part of our Lord's own words to Nicodemus; and this gives them an emphasized note-worthiness for certain reasons which we shall proceed to mention.

First, we see in them *our Lord's unmistakable seal upon the veracity and Divine inspiration of the Old Testament.* When our Lord referred Nicodemus away back to the uplifted serpent of brass in Numbers xxi, He was indicating His own acceptance

of its historicity. We cannot bring ourselves to believe that He
was referring to it merely as an item in legendary folk-lore. He
gives not even the semblance of a hint that the thing may not
actually have happened.

There are those to-day, however, who occupy "high places"
in the Christian world, who scorn to believe that the incident
ever occurred as related in the Book of Numbers. Some say it
never happened at all. Others say that the account of it is a
mythical exaggeration, a "heightening into the miraculous" of
something which was quite *non*-miraculous when it actually
happened. And there are thousands calling themselves Christians
to-day who follow these leaders, and swallow such scepticisms
as the "findings of modern scholarship."

Peake's *Commentary*, for instance, speaks of the account as
"an instance of sympathetic magic inverted," or "an aitiological
legend to explain the practice of serpent-worship."

This raises at once the whole matter of our Lord's attitude to
the Old Testament. Has He made His attitude really clear? He has.

Our Lord's attitude to the Old Testament may be resolved
into the following three propositions: (1) He was always quoting
it, but He never once queried it. (2) He always quoted it in
such a way as to endorse it. (3) He endorsed the whole of it as
the inspired word of God.

CONTINUOUS REFERENCE

Almost the first thing that strikes us about our Lord's preaching and teaching is His continuous reference and deference to
the Old Testament. From the very outset of His ministry, when
He defeated the Tempter with that thrice-uttered "It is written,"
right on to His last word from the Cross, "Father, into Thy
hands I commend My spirit" (see Ps. xxxi. 5), He was quoting,
explaining, appropriating, or otherwise using, one part or another
of the Old Testament Scriptures.

He did not merely quote from the Old Testament in a general
way. He mentioned particular writers and characters and institutions and incidents by name. Yet He never gave the faintest

hint of doubt or query or uncertainty. Of course, He recognised
that much in the Mosaic economy was imperfect and provisional,
and that in at least one instance it was even concessional, as
when, in Matthew xix. 8, He told the Pharisees: "Moses, because
of the hardness of your hearts suffered you to put away your
wives" (though note His immediately added words, "*But from
the beginning it was not so,*" indicating that the concession was
not the voice of the Old Testament ethic as a whole). Our Lord
knew that in certain of its social regulations the Mosaic legisla-
tion was only the best *provisionally*; yet this in no way modifies
His acceptance of the whole as being from God, stamped with
Divine authority, and making known the Divine mind and will.

To contend, as some do, that our Lord repudiated certain
moral standards of the Old covenant when He said, in the Sermon
on the Mount, "But *I* say unto you . . ." is a superficiality
of reasoning which is unworthy of honest scholarship. Look up
the six verses (Matt. v. 21, 27, 31, 33, 38, 43). Careful consideration will show that our Lord, other than abrogating these precepts,
intensified their meaning, insisting that they were meant to be
honoured, not merely by an outward observance, but in inward
motive as well.

Take the one which has been seized on most of all: "An eye
for an eye, and a tooth for a tooth." A mere glance back at the
Book of Exodus will show that this ruling was given to Israel's
magistrates, to see that fair play was meted out to both parties
in a dispute. It was never given to *individuals*, meaning that as
individuals they should *personally* exact "an eye for an eye, and
a tooth for a tooth"! Our Lord's words, however, in the Sermon
on the Mount *are* to individuals as such. When He says, "Whosoever shall smite thee on thy right cheek, turn to him the other
also," He is telling us that although we *may* claim "an eye for
an eye" as a matter of administrative justice, we ought rather
to suffer injury meekly.

Why, to make out that our Lord is here abrogating the com-
mands of the Old Testament makes Him contradict the very
words with which He introduces His references to them: "Whosoever, therefore, shall break one of these least commandments,
and shall teach men so, he shall be called least in the kingdom

of heaven" (verse 19). The fact is, our Lord's whole attitude to the Old Testament may be summed up in His words which just precede verse 19: "Think not that I am come to destroy the Law or the Prophets. I am not come to destroy, but to fulfil. For verily I say unto you, Till heaven and earth pass away, one jot or one tittle shall in no wise pass from the Law till all be fulfilled."

UNIFORM ENDORSEMENT

Our Lord frequently condemns the errors of the Jews or the misconceptions of His disciples, but never once does He utter anything but endorsement for the Old Testament scriptures. Whenever He mentions Old Testament incidents or characters or institutions or authorships, He does so in such language as makes clear His own belief in their genuineness. Pages might be filled, giving illustrations of all this. All we can do here is to pick out one or two as representative.

Take that incident which has been scouted more than any other by the "New Theology" advocates, the story of Jonah. We are asked to believe that our Lord merely referred to it as any of ourselves might refer for illustration's sake to a fictitious character in Bunyan's *Pilgrim's Progress*, without meaning at all to imply real historicity. But careful note of our Lord's words tears any such argument to shreds. He says: "The men of Nineveh shall rise in the judgment with this generation, and shall condemn it, because they repented at the preaching of Jonas; and behold a greater than Jonas is here." If the Book of Jonah is not historically true, then the incarnate Son of God is here teaching that fictitious persons who are supposed to have repented at the fictitious preaching of a fictitious prophet in a fictitious story will yet rise up and stand in the actual judgment and condemn those men who were our Lord's actual hearers! To charge our Lord with such trifling is monstrous effrontery.

We cite just one more instance out of the many. It has to do with the Davidic authorship of Psalm cx. The "modern" verdict, so we are told, is that this psalm was not written until centuries later than David, and certainly not by a king. But observe our

Lord's question about it to the Pharisees: "How then doth *David* in the *Spirit* call Him (i.e. the coming Messiah) Lord?" All in this one reference our Lord acknowledges (1) the presence of supernatural prediction in the Old Testament, i.e. David's having written of something over a thousand years in advance; (2) the fact of special Divine inspiration, for He says that David wrote "in the Spirit"; (3) the Messianic element in the Book of the Psalms, for He says that David was writing of the Christ or Messiah; (4) the Davidic authorship of the psalm being quoted.

Ironically enough, it is Christ versus the modern critics far more than Christ versus the old-time Pharisees; for on all these points the Pharisees completely concurred with Him.

INSPIRATION UNIQUE AND PLENARY

But we may go on to say that our Lord endorses the inspiration of the Old Testament as being *unique* and *verbal* and *total*. It is an inspiration which lifts these Scriptures up above all other writings, as having an authority found nowhere else. We see this in the way He uniformly submits and appeals to them. While He admits no binding authority even in the "Traditions of the Elders," the word of Scripture itself is always final; and the ascribing of such superhuman finality *implies* Divine inspiration.

But general implication can easily be supplemented by many particular statements from the lips of our Lord. For illustration, we pick one instance only. In Mark vii. 8, 9, 13, He thus reproves the Pharisees: "Laying aside the commandment of God, ye hold the tradition of men. . . . Full well ye reject the commandment of God, that ye may keep your own tradition." Here, our Lord, in quoting from the Old Testament, twice calls it, "*the commandment of God*," and once, "the *word* of God." Can such phraseology mean less than Divine inspiration? And this is the kind of phraseology our Lord uses continually.

Equally clearly does He witness that the inspiration of the Old Testament is *verbal*. In His first-recorded public discourse He says: "Till heaven and earth pass, *one jot or one tittle shall in no wise pass from the Law.*" "Whosoever shall break *one of*

these least commandments . . ." In Matthew xxii. 31, 32, His
reply to the Sadducees hangs even on the tense of a verb, as
He quotes Exodus iii. 6, "I *am* the God of Abraham"; not
merely "was," but "*am*"! If these and all the other instances
which might be cited do not make clear that our Lord looked
upon the Old Testament as verbally inspired, we are strangely
mistaken.

But crowningly, our Lord seals the inspiration of the Old
Testament as being *total*. He knows nothing of "degrees" of
inspiration, or "qualitative" inspiration. To Him the Old Testament is a unity. He quotes from its different parts with equal
deference and equal confidence. He refers to the three main
book-groups of the Old Testament, the "Law," and the "Prophets," and the "Psalms," as being of equal sacredness and
authority. Here again we might give a number of examples,
but we pick just one, which, in our own judgment, is so *in*clusive
as to become quite *con*clusive. In Luke xxiv. 44, our Lord says:

"These are the words which I spake unto you while I was yet
with you, that all things must be fulfilled which were written
in the LAW of Moses, and in the PROPHETS, and in the
PSALMS concerning ME."

These are words spoken by our Lord after His resurrection.
If then there were limits to His knowledge *before* His resurrection (as some would tell us), such limits are certainly discarded
now! Note, then, that the risen Christ endorses all three parts
of the Old Testament—the "Law," and the "Prophets," and
the "Psalms." Note, also, that it is "all things which were
WRITTEN"; so it is the actual writings to which He refers.
Note, again, that in all three parts there is the Messianic and
prophetic element—"all things which were written . . . concerning ME." This prophetic element is always the unmistakable
seal of Divine inspiration. And, once more, note the word,
"must"—"all things MUST be fulfilled." Why that "must"?
Because the Law and the Prophets and the Psalms are alike of
Divine origin, and therefore cannot possibly be in error. If such
words as these are not a seal of Christ upon the inspiration of
the Old Testament in total, what *could* be?

Such, then, is our Lord's attitude to the Old Testament. Freely and fully, clearly and decisively, He endorses the whole of it as the inspired word of God.

BUT IS CHRIST'S WITNESS VALID?

To some of us it may sound almost blasphemous to ask: *Is Christ's witness valid?* But the question is forced on us by others. Critics of the Modernist school try to discount our Lord's witness by sponsoring two theories, known respectively as the *Kenosis* theory, and the *accommodation* theory.

The "Kenosis" Theory.

This theory is so called from the verb (ekenosen) which Paul uses in Philippians ii. 7. Strictly translated it is, "He emptied Himself" (see A.S.V.). It is argued from this that our Lord so "emptied Himself" in His becoming man as to make Himself practically subject to ordinary human limitation of knowledge. He had no knowledge beyond that of His contemporaries as to the origins, authorship, and literary characteristics of the Scriptures. He shared the opinions of His countrymen on such topics, even when they were in error.

But the theory is a mere shell without a kernel. The more one honestly tests it, the more it falls to bits.

Glance back at the "kenosis" passage, Philippians ii. 5–8. Is it not obvious that the meaning of "He emptied Himself" is determined by the word "*form*," which comes just before it and again just after it, as if to guard it from possible misunderstanding? We are told of One who was in the "*form* of God," who took the "*form* of a bondman." As plainly as can be, the contrast which Paul here makes is not the contrast between being God and then being something less, but the contrast between being in the "form" of God and then being in the "form" of a bondman. Now that word "form" in the Greek is *morphe*. According to Liddell and Scott's *Greek Lexicon* it means "form, shape, figure, fashion, appearance." So the word has certainly nothing to do with the *nature* or *essence* either of our Lord's deity or of

His humanity. Our Lord only "emptied Himself" in the sense of changing the *expression* of His being.

It is a strange marvel that men who sneer at "verbal inspiration" should make so much of one single word as they do in connection with their "kenosis" theory; but it is no surprise that they should make such an exegetical *blunder* in interpreting that word, for a determination to press a theory at all costs always warps the mind.

But then the whole data of the four Gospels is also against the Modernist "kenosis" theory. In the opening paragraphs of the fourth Gospel we have the Johannine equivalent to the Pauline "kenosis" passage. A careful study of it shows it to be the best of all commentaries on the Philippian passage, and it utterly refutes the new-fangled "self-emptying" hypothesis. We here quote simply one statement from it: "And the Word became flesh . . . FULL of grace and TRUTH" (verse 14). No "kenosis" *there*!—not in the "higher critical" sense, at any rate.

And all over the four Gospels there are indications that the mentality of the Lord Jesus had no such limits as the "kenosis" theorists would make out. The immortal third chapter of John is introduced with the words: "Jesus . . . *knew all men*, and needed not that any should testify of man; for He *knew what was in man*." We think of His telling the woman of Sychar, whom He had never met before, all about her past, and of a score of similar incidents all proving that instead of mental limits there is a strange and wonderful *freedom* from normal human limits. Or we think of our Lord's predictions concerning both the near and the distant future; and again, instead of limits to His knowledge, we see that there is a supernatural and even Divine *un*limitedness.

Or, still more, we recall some of His pronouncements concerning *Himself*. Several times He appropriates to Himself the Jehovistic "I AM" (John viii. 24, Eng. R.V. margin). For this the Jews sought to stone Him. We hear Him say, "I am THE TRUTH"; and can we think that He who says this with such august simplicity and reality was self-deceived, fallible, and even gullible? Could HE make all sorts of slips about the Old Testament? For the modern "scholar" to say that our Lord's knowledge "did not necessarily extend to questions of literary criticism" is simply throwing dust into the air. Listen to *these* words, which make modern criticism seem petty by comparison: "*Heaven and earth shall pass away, but My words shall not pass away.*" Is there any suggestion of limitedness or uncertainty *there*?

Such words as we find in Luke ii. 40 and 52, that the child Jesus "increased in wisdom and stature," are not really relevant to the point at issue; for it is not with the "*child*" Jesus, but with the Jesus of the public ministry and teaching that we are concerned. Nor does that supposed "trump card" of the "kenosis" theorists, Mark xiii. 52, serve them any better: "Of that day and that hour knoweth no man, no, not the angels which are in heaven, *neither the Son*, but the Father." In that very verse our Lord lifts His knowledge above that of both "man" and "angels," and calls Himself by that title which more than any other implies His deity—"THE SON"; and all that with reference to Himself while still in the flesh! That is the very *opposite* of "kenosis" in the Modernist sense!

Neither facts nor reason support the "kenosis" theory. Our Lord certainly could not "empty Himself" *of* Himself! And the overwhelming evidence of the Gospels is not an emptiedness down to normal human limits, but a super-normal *fulness* of knowledge. The "kenosis" theory is a "broken cistern that can hold no water." Our Lord's witness to the Old Testament remains as valid and final as on the day He said, "Heaven and earth shall pass away, but My words shall not pass away."

"*Accommodation*" *Theory*.

Another way of trying to circumvent the witness of Christ to the inspiration of the Old Testament is the disloyal and unworthy argument that He *accommodated* His teaching to the ignorance of the people in general and the traditional misconceptions of their religious teachers. It was unnecessary to disturb their minds on literary questions which had no importance at that time and no real relevance to the "religious mission of Jesus"; and it was equally desirable as far as possible to avoid arousing unnecessary opposition on the part of the religious leaders. So He withheld much that He might otherwise have said.

Such is the gist of the argument, but it is as mentally untenable as it is morally unworthy. As we carefully consider how cruelly it reflects upon the stainless character and guileless lips of our glorious Saviour, with all the united weight of New Testament evidence against it, we cannot but feel quite as warmly and strongly as the writer of the following words. "That Abraham, Moses, Peter, or even Paul, might *fall* after this fashion is conceivable, for at their best they were only errant mortals; but to whisper such a suggestion about our all-perfect and spotlessly-transparent Redeemer is nothing short of an impious libel, and a base calumny upon His reputation. No *honest* man could act thus; and to admit such a thought concerning our Divine Lord 'who knew no sin, neither was guile found in His mouth,' is to degrade Him to the level of a shifty, trimming Jesuit, and, in so thieving away His character, to rob us of our Saviour."

Let any honest-minded reader go through the pages which narrate our Lord's ministry, right from that fearless "Sermon on the Mount" to the final "Woe unto you, Scribes and Pharisees, hypocrites!" and the fearful death which our Saviour's uncompromising exposure of sin and error brought upon Him, and there will be no need of words from ourselves to disprove the "accommodation" pretext. Surely our "new schools" of Bible teachers would never have lowered themselves to such a shameless shift if their other arguments to discount our Lord's seal on the Old Testament had not proved such an intellectual failure.

As is well known, during the past hundred years the documents of our New Testament and especially of the Gospels have been subjected to the fiercest testing of critical "criticism" in all their history. At one point or another, by one big-sounding scholar or another, they have been doubted, scouted, and flouted— yet where is the scholarly critic to-day who would deny that these documents have survived the seven-times-heated furnace? At the very least, we are obliged to accept them as substantially genuine and true; and there is ample reason to accept them as being altogether and absolutely so.

Well, if we do, there can be no doubt whatever that the incarnate King of Kings and Lord of Lords has put His own unmistakable imprimatur upon the inspiration of the Old Testament as being unique and verbal and total. And our contention is that His seal ought to be the decisive factor with all who call Him "Lord."

We ourselves accept His word as final, and praise God for it. When we *do* accept His witness, a revealing ray from heaven reaches back over the pages of the Old Testament. Its prophecy and typology and all its latent Christology irradiate new and thrilling outshinings of Divine revelation for us. Those who grope about amid the usual loose Modernist ideas of "inspiration" are blind to all such meaning in the Old Testament. Years ago now, Sir Robert Anderson wrote: "The leaders in this Higher Criticism crusade have facile pens and they are prolific authors. And yet if they may be judged by their writings, there is not one of them who is a student of prophetic truth or of the typology of Scripture." They are self-blinded to the choicest riches of Old Testament teaching!

We have one more word to add. It is wonderful how *the Bible confirms itself* to those who accept it as our Lord accepted it. For instance, our Lord clearly accepted the historicity of the Jonah story. We ourselves therefore accept it too. What then? Why, this: away back in 2 Kings xiv. 25, we find a direct historical reference to this same "Jonah, the son of Amittai" in the reign of Jeroboam II, proving that he was indeed a real personage. Our Lord also clearly accepted the genuineness of Daniel and the book which bears his name. We ourselves therefore accept it too. What then? Why, this: away back in Ezekiel (the one book of the prophets against the genuineness of which even the "higher critics" have never been able to make a case!), in chapter xiv. 14, 20, we find a mention of Daniel as being outstandingly known at that very time in Babylonia, *the time of Nebuchadnezzar*, completely disproving the theory of the Modernists that Daniel is merely a pseudepigraphical document of the time of Antiochus Epiphanes, four hundred years later!

And so it is with the incident of the uplifted brazen serpent away back in Numbers xxi, to which our Lord refers in John iii. 14.

Our Lord clearly accepted the historicity of this incident. We ourselves therefore accept it. What then? Why, this: away back in 2 Kings xviii. 4, we find a strange yet illuminating reference to this very serpent of brass, in the reign of good king Hezekiah, which absolutely settles the fact of its actual existence—

"He (King Hezekiah) removed the high places, and brake the images, and cut down the groves, and BRAKE IN PIECES THE BRAZEN SERPENT THAT MOSES HAD MADE: for unto those days the children of Israel did burn incense to it. And it was called Nehushtan (i.e. the little brass thing)."

The brass serpent had become a religious relic which the people were now superstitiously venerating, so Hezekiah wisely had it destroyed. But the point we make here is that *there it was— seven hundred years after Moses!*

It is on this incident that the great declaration of John iii. 16 is founded. It was no mere bit of "sympathetic magic inverted," as the high-faluting lingo of the Modernist commentator categorises it! The decisive imprimatur of the King Himself seals its genuineness for us! And in it there is not only historical reality, but a wonderful wealth of typological significance. This we shall explore in some measure in our following studies.

OLD TESTAMENT TYPOLOGY

Out from the heart of nature rolled
The burdens of the Bible old;
The litanies of nations came
Like the volcano's tongue of flame
Up from the burning core below—
The canticles of love and woe.
The word unto the prophets spoken
Was writ on tablets yet unbroken;
Still floats upon the morning wind,
Still whispers to the willing mind;
One accent of the Holy Ghost
The heedless world has never lost.

Emerson

OLD TESTAMENT TYPOLOGY

Look again at these words about the uplifted serpent of brass in John iii. 14, 15. They imply the fact of *Old Testament typology*. One of the most wonderful phenomena of the Old Testament Scriptures is their latent typological content. Instances of this are cited repeatedly in the New Testament. For instance, in Romans v. 14, we read: "Adam . . . is a figure of Him that was to come." So Adam was a type of Christ (for the Greek word translated as "figure" is *tupos*, from which our English word "type" comes). Similarly, in Hebrews vii. 3, Melchizedek is said to have been "made like unto," or more exactly, *made to resemble* the Son of God.

But besides the fact that *persons*, like Adam and Melchizedek, are types, we find that many *objects* also are types. In 1 Corinthians x. 4, Paul writes: "That rock (i.e. of which the Israelites drank, as recorded in Exodus xvii) was Christ." And in Hebrews ix. 8, 9, we are told that the old Israelite Tabernacle was a *parabole* (i.e. a parable or comparison) of spiritual truths revealed centuries later, in the New Testament.

Then again, besides persons and objects, even *events* may be types. In 1 Peter iii. 21, we read that Noah's being "saved" through the Flood was a transition of which the baptism of Christian believers is now the spiritual *antitupos* or "antitype"; while in Hebrews xi. 19, we are told that Abraham's receiving back of victim-Isaac from the altar on Mount Moriah was a *parabole* or simile of resurrection.

Thus we see that persons, objects and events may all be invested with this latent typical meaning. What is more, there are passages in the New Testament which categorically affirm the *general* presence of types in the Old Testament Scriptures. There is no mistaking pronouncements like that in 1 Corinthians x. 11, "All these things happened unto them as *tupoi* (types)." That covers

all the way from Egypt to Canaan! And Hebrews x. 1 tells us
that the whole of the Law was a "shadow (i.e. a dark outline
or silhouette) of things to come"!

Moreover, there are other chapters and verses in our New
Testament which, although they do not *state* the fact that such
type-teaching is found up and down the Old Testament, obviously
imply it. We think of our Lord's great discourse on the Manna,
in John vi; of Paul's contrastive exposition of the two ministrations, the "Letter" verses the "Spirit," in 2 Corinthians iii–iv;
of the argument based upon the typical significance of Isaac
and Ishmael, in Galatians iv; of the Melchizedek and Aaron
passages in the epistle to the Hebrews; of our Lord's reference
to Jonah's three days inside the great fish; and of many another
such example; and we cannot fail to see that our Lord's reference to the brazen serpent, in John iii. 14, 15, is but one among
many indications of this wonderful mystery which inheres in
the Old Testament.

And still further, even if we did not have either these *ex*plicit
or *im*plicit New Testament warrants for our belief in the latent
typology of the Old Testament, the circumstantial data in some
cases are such that we simply could not fail to see the presence of
typical meanings. The correspondences between the Old Testament types and the New Testament antitypes are too many and
too exact to be explained as mere coincidences. We are nowhere
told, for instance, that *Joseph* is a type of *Christ*, yet who can
read those immortal old Genesis chapters without seeing in
Joseph, first as the beloved son of his father, then as the rejected
and exiled of his brethren, and then as the prince and saviour
exalted to the throne as the world's bread-supplier—who can
read it all without perceiving in Joseph one of the clearest and
fullest types of Christ anywhere in the Scriptures?

Our Lord and His apostles both assume and assert this presence
of types in the Old Testament. Such a warrant, coming to us
from the Spirit of inspiration Himself through the lips of Christ
and the pens of the inspired New Testament writers is enough
to settle the matter conclusively so far as we ourselves are concerned.

But what precisely *is* a type? A type may be said to be any person, event, act, or institution, Divinely adapted to represent some spiritual reality or to prefigure some person or truth to be revealed later. Or, in other words, God has been pleased to invest certain persons, objects, events, acts, institutions, with a prefigurative meaning, so that besides having a real relationship with their own times, they have contained a significance reaching far forward into the future.

VALUES OF TYPOLOGY

Few people, alas, seem to realise the unique and priceless values of this typological lore in the Old Testament. Think of its *evidential* value. It is unquestionably the supreme proof of Divine inspiration. If this typical import does indeed inhere, then how unanswerably it demonstrates superhuman wisdom and foreknowledge! For, remember, not only do the Old Testament types exhibit the consummate skill of the Divine Workman, but they are a form of *prophecy*, forepicturing persons and things which were yet to be, and revealing the Divine anticipation of future events. Now, as we have said already, prophecy such as we have in the Old Testament—in such abundance and detail, and in such exact, arresting and unmistakable fulfilment—is a proof of inspiration before which the keenest and ablest opponents of Christianity have been silenced.

The fact is, the argument from fulfilled prophecy is unanswerable, and no really unprejudiced student can examine the facts without becoming permanently convinced thereby. "This is the finger of God!" However clever twentieth-century man may be in many ways, there is one thing which he is still absolutely incapable of doing, and will always remain incapable of doing, and that is, to know or tell or determine the future. That is something which neither men nor angels can do, neither crystal-gazers nor spiritist mediums, neither demons nor the devil himself. Only GOD can know the future, for the simple, final reason that He alone sovereignly *predetermines* the future.

In the Old Testament we have hundreds of prophecies, written hundreds of years before the events foretold, all of which have been fulfilled to the very letter. God Himself *offers* this marvel of evidence to all who will receive it. But however wonderful, plainly-stated and unfiguratively expressed prediction may be, *the most wonderful of all kinds of prophecy is* TYPOLOGICAL PROPHECY. To refer to Joseph again as a type of Christ, is it not a simply matchless marvel to see all the outstanding features of our Lord's first and second comings anticipatively and illustratively *enacted* before us in the personal character and history of Joseph? Or, to refer to the sweet savour offerings and the non-sweet savour offerings detailed in the first seven chapters of Leviticus, is it not a profoundly astonishing pheno-menon that away back there, fifteen hundred years before the birth of our Lord, all the different aspects of His death on Calvary should be successively distinguished and emphasised by those different offerings which were enjoined on the Israelites?

Such types are indeed the most wonderful form of prophecy; for not only do they most wonderfully reveal the depthless genius of the inspiring Spirit, and at the same time wonderfully exhibit the sovereignly manipulating control of God in human affairs, but they give a colour, a fulness, and a vividness of pre-sentation which cannot be given in plainly-stated, unfigurative prediction. There is absolutely no accounting for them but by the one word, GOD. They are a simply unanswerable evidence of the fact that the Old Testament is the inspired word of God.

But besides this evidential value of Old Testament typology, there is its *spiritual* value. This cannot easily be over-stated. These many and various types have a strange and fascinating spell about them. They make the truth live and move, and glow and grow, and walk and talk, before our very eyes—and that, centuries in advance of their fulfilment! Moreover, we go back to them again and again, and continually discover in them new turns of meaning, new significances and relevances, so that they are a never-ending vein of wealth. There is a reciprocal effect between these Old Testament types and their New Testament fulfilments. The fulfilments of the New interpret the types of the Old, and the types of the Old illumine the doctrines of the New. The types of the Old Testament are like the reflection of the sun from a many-coloured window.

There is such a wealth of meaning in them that we cannot but deeply regret the neglect of them in the new approach to the Bible. In some quarters, too, the study of the types has fallen into disfavour because allegorical and mystical interpretations have been carried to foolish extravagances which are without any New Testament warrant whatever. Studied with good sense and a careful eye to New Testament teaching, the typology of the Old Testament is a priceless treasure-mine to the Bible student, and should on no account be neglected.

Why, to take only the first book of the Old Testament, what wealth of latent type-teaching we find *there*! Think of the typical *persons* in Genesis: Adam, a type of Christ; Eve, a type of the Church; Cain and Abel, a type of the carnal versus the spiritual; Enoch, a type of the coming Translation; the survivors of the Flood, a type of the deliverance from the coming tribulation and judgment to a "new heaven and a new earth"; Lot, a type of the so-called "worldly" believer; Melchizedek, a type of Christ as King-Priest; Hagar and Sarah, a type of Law versus Grace; Ishmael and Isaac, a type of the "flesh" versus the Spirit; Abraham and Isaac on Mount Moriah, a type of God the Father and Christ the Son in relation to Calvary; Isaac, Rebecca and the servant, a type of Christ and the Church and the Holy Spirit; Joseph, a type of Christ; and Asenath, a type of the Church.

Or take the typical *objects* and *events* in Genesis: the sun, a type of Christ; the moon, a type of the Church; the six days, a type of spiritual regeneration; the Sabbath, a type of spiritual rest; the "coats" which God gave to Adam and Eve, a type of imputed righteousness; Abel's lamb, a type of the Lamb of Calvary; the Flood, a type of the coming judgment; the ark, a type of Christ; the raven and the dove, a type (or at least a striking illustration) of the old nature versus the new, in the believer; the Sodom fire-storm, a type of the "wrath to come"; Egypt a type of "this present evil world."

PRINCIPLES OF INTERPRETATION

Just because the typology of the Old Testament is so wonderful, however, it is a precious lore which must be guarded from wrong use. In our interpretation and application of types there are two precautions which should always be borne in mind. First: no doctrine or theory should ever be built upon a type or types independently of direct teaching elsewhere in Scripture. Types are meant to amplify and vivify doctrine, but not to originate it. They are illuminative but not foundational. Their purpose is to illustrate not formulate.

This is obvious in the very nature of the case, for if they are types, then they are not originals, but representations of things other than themselves; and unless the realities which they typify existed, the types themselves could not exist. Thus, types are dependent and must not be used independently to authenticate doctrine.

Some time ago we heard a preacher advocating an elaborate theory that at the second coming of Christ the saints must pass through successive heavens, to undergo a process of purification before being presented at the throne of God, the whole theory being construed from a passage of somewhat doubtful import in Leviticus. That sort of thing is wrong, and should be guarded against.

Nor should the parallelism between the Old Testament type and the New Testament antitype be pressed to fanciful extremes. Types, it would seem, are not meant so much to be exact and minute replicas of those things which they typify as rather to enrich and illumine our understanding of the more essential features in the antitype. When the interpretation of types is carried into insignificant minutiae, it degenerates into an imaginative allegorising which has many dangers.

All these thoughts are in our mind as once again our eyes linger over the words of John iii. 14, 15—

"And as Moses lifted up the serpent in the wilderness, even so must the Son of Man be lifted up, that whosoever believeth in Him should not perish, but have everlasting life."

As the context in John iii shows, that uplifted serpent of brass is one of the many great Old Testament types; and, as we now turn to consider it more particularly, we shall find it flashing a heavenly illumination upon the Cross of our Lord and Saviour, Jesus Christ.

AWAY BACK TO NUMBERS!

At a House Dinner of the Authors' Club, I was seated, to my great pleasure, next to my old Oxford coach, Professor Sayce. In the course of conversation I remarked how strange it was that a number of our clergy had lost faith in the historical character of the Old Testament. He said: *"They are behind the times."* I thought that coming from a man like Sayce, who knew what he was talking about, the remark deserved to be remembered.

Rev. A. C. Downer, D.D.

AWAY BACK TO NUMBERS!

IT HAS been truly said that the best illustrations of New Testament doctrine are those which we find in Old Testament story. Nor is it surprising that this should be so, for the Old and New Testaments of our Bible are one interwoven whole. As Augustine said, the New is latent in the Old, and the Old is patent in the New. Or as another has put it, the New is *en*folded in the Old, and the Old is *un*folded in the New. Every major doctrine of the New Testament is matched by some illuminating type, figure, incident or institution somewhere in the Old Testament.

For instance, if we would find the perfect illustration of "walking in the light" and being "cleansed from all sin" by the blood of the Lord Jesus, we must turn to Leviticus with its seventeen chapters on cleansing by sacrifice and its remaining ten chapters on practical sanctity. Or, if we want the best illustration of possessing our possessions in the "heavenly places" in Christ, as taught in Ephesians, we must turn back to the book of Joshua and see Israel first entering and then subduing and then occupying the earthly Canaan. Or would we illustrate how the Gospel saves the sinner? Where is there a more graphic delineation than the cleansing of leprous Naaman in Jordan? Do we want the really classic exemplification of the principles upon which faith works and waits and wars and wins? Then we must hark back to the conquest of Jericho. If we want the superb vivification of what it means to be "more than conquerors through Him that loved us," we must turn back to the epic of David and Goliath, and see stripling David not only slaying Goliath with that first stone, but having the four more stones ready to deal with Goliath's four giant-brothers who also were in the Philistine army!

Even so, if we would best see for ourselves, and best show to others, how salvation and eternal life come to the repentant sinner by believing on the Lord Jesus Christ, we must turn away back to the Book of Numbers, to the account of the uplifted serpent of brass which saved all the serpent-bitten Israelites who looked to it. This is the illustration which our Lord Jesus Himself used to the religiously educated but spiritually unenlightened Nicodemus, with telling power. And the very fact that our Lord thus singled it out invests it with a peculiar noteworthiness. So, then, we turn away back to Numbers, to the twenty-first chapter, verses 4 to 9.

> "And they journeyed from Mount Hor by the way of the Red Sea, to compass the land of Edom; and the soul of the people was much discouraged because of the way.
>
> "And the people spake against God and against Moses: Wherefore have ye brought us up out of Egypt to die in the wilderness? for there is no bread, neither is there any water, and our soul loatheth this light bread.
>
> "And the Lord sent fiery serpents among the people, and they bit the people; and much people of Israel died.
>
> "Therefore the people came to Moses and said: We have sinned, for we have spoken against the Lord and against thee; pray unto the Lord that He take away the serpents from us. And Moses prayed for the people.
>
> "And the Lord said unto Moses: Make thee a fiery serpent, and set it upon a pole; and it shall come to pass that every one that is bitten, when he looketh upon it shall live.
>
> "And Moses made a serpent of brass, and put it upon a pole; and it came to pass that if a serpent had bitten any man, when he beheld the serpent of brass, he lived."

There is the type in its setting. We are eager to examine that uplifted metal serpent, for it is rich with evangelical significances; yet even in the *setting*, apart from the type itself, there is a tremendous fourfold truth which we ought not to pass over without at least a brief consideration. In fact, we *cannot* pass it lightly, for it at once arrests our attention.

It is the fourfold progress in the incident—sin, suffering, supplication, salvation. Mark it well:

SIN

"The people spake against God and against Moses . . ."

SUFFERING

"And the Lord sent fiery serpents among the people . . ."

SUPPLICATION

"We have sinned. Pray unto the Lord that He take away the serpents . . ."

SALVATION

"Make thee a fiery serpent, and set it upon a pole; and it shall come to pass that every one that is bitten, when he looketh upon it, shall live."

These four components go in two inseparable pairs—(1) sinning and suffering; (2) supplication and salvation. And what God hath joined together no man can put asunder!

SINNING AND SUFFERING

This inseparable union of sinning and suffering is a truth *which many people willingly forget*; but it is only too real, as all such foolish ignorers of it discover sooner or later to their cost. That venturesome-spirited young worldling thinks he can laugh spiritual concerns out of his life and have his full fling of fleshly follies without any suffering afterwards. That voluptuous young fellow thinks he can sow his wild oats without reaping a wild harvest. That attractive young daughter of Eve thinks she can take fire into her bosom and not be burned. How many there are who, either from pitiful superficiality or wilful self-deception, go on in evil courses, foolishly imagining that somehow they can dodge any aftermath of suffering! What a costly delusion this is! You cannot dandle the deadly viper without its fangs biting into your flesh and its fiery venom getting into your blood. As surely as the godless Dives lifted up his eyes amid the torments of Hades, so surely do those who go on in ways of sin wake up, sooner or later, on a bed of flames.

The *denial* of this connection between sinning and suffering is one of Satan's favourite subterfuges in the deceiving of human beings. If only he can persuade men and women that they may sin without fear of suffering, he knows they will then sin with impunity and excess. If only he can blindfold our inward eyes to the danger-signal of conscience, he can lead us where he will. But Satan is a liar. He himself knows well enough that as truly as the law of gravitation operates throughout the physical universe, so does this law by which suffering follows sinning operate throughout the moral realm. Satan himself is powerless to escape its inexorable action. The lake of unquenchable fire which finally engulfs him is the inevitable creation of his own monstrous sinning.

Of course, the connection between sinning and suffering is *not always apparent*. Yet even where this is so, the connection is none the less a certainty. God is not mocked. The moral laws which condition the universe never break down and never deviate a hair's breadth from the line of exact retribution. A man may sometimes recognise in his suffering the direct consequence of former sin; and indeed many persons who suffer in later life *do* perceive that their blasted paradises are the outcome of previous folly. But even where sin is not so plainly followed by such exactments, this law of reaping according to the sowing is unsuspectedly working itself out. The Latin poet, Horace, has a couplet to the effect that Vengeance, although "lame on one foot" seldom fails in the end to "overtake his quarry." I have read of a man who was stricken down with blindness when scarcely past middle life. He wondered why such a dire deprivation should have befallen him, for there was no tendency of that kind anywhere in his family. He never knew; but his doctor did. His sightless eyes were the result of one dark sin committed long before, in college days. In citing such an example we are not within a million miles of suggesting that others who suffer similar affliction are paying penalty for similar sin, or even for any sin of their own at all. The man we have mentioned is one individual only, and perhaps a unique case; yet he serves as a sad illustration of the truth that long-forgotten sin, and sin which seems to have left no deposit of suffering whatever, has its inevitable and inexorable processes and consequences in our being.

A man hears the voice of God's Spirit in his soul, pleading with him to accept Christ as Saviour, but his reaction is a deliberate "No" to God. Well, that sin is seen by none but God, and it seems to have no mentionable effect at the time. Perhaps the same thing has happened with him several times before, seemingly without any deleterious consequence. But if we think that such a person really is no different after such refusal, we are wrong. See that same person, years afterward, suddenly waking up to the emptiness of life without God, or facing some emergency destitute of all sense of God's presence, or crying out as death draws near, "Oh, that I knew where I might find Him! Oh, how I wish I had not resisted God's Spirit years ago! I thought I could easily turn to God later; but, alas, I cannot repent now; my heart will not turn; the Holy Spirit's strivings have ceased; my heart is cold, and now heaven seems brass; and somehow I cannot now seek God as I thought I would, for my very nature seems to have become set and hard and distant from Him!" Yes, even where the processes are invisible, this law of cause and effect operates between sinning and suffering. And what begins and developes in time goes on in the life beyond this one.

When we reflect upon it, we soon conclude that sinning and suffering *must* go together as a matter of moral necessity. It is inconceivable that it should be otherwise. But for this dread law the universe would be a moral chaos; heaven and hell would lose all separate meaning in one vast inferno.

Again, it is well to be reminded that in the operation of this law there are no freaks. There is an infallible principle of deadly accuracy and poetic exactness, so that the suffering corresponds with an exquisite equality to the sinning.

And what is the greatest sin of all? It is that of knowingly and impenitently flaunting the saving love of God in Jesus Christ. It may not seem so when considered from merely social or criminal viewpoints; but when we reflect on the state of heart which it reveals, we begin to perceive the enormity of it. There is a sharp difference between a *non*-believer and an *un*believer. The millions of heathen who have never heard even the name of Jesus are *non*-believers, but they are not *un*believers, for they have not rejected the Lord Jesus. They have never had the chance of accepting, and therefore have never incurred the guilt of rejecting. They are neither believers nor unbelievers; they are *non*-believers; and at death the souls of such pass into Hades to await the day of general judgment at the Great White Throne (Rev. xx. 11–15). But those who really know the Gospel and understandingly refuse it are *un*believers; and the word of Scripture forewarns all such that before ever the judgment at the Great White Throne takes place they are "condemned already." John iii. 18 says, "He that believeth not is condemned already," or as Weymouth translates it, "has already received sentence." The awful sin of rejecting Christ is no mere isolated act; it is the expression of a *condition* into which impenitence has brought the heart. The more one carefully thinks of it, so the more deeply is the mind impressed that no sin conceivable could be more terrible than that of trampling underfoot the "love so amazing, so Divine" which poured itself out for our sakes in the mingling blood and tears and atoning expiations of Calvary.

And the very mention of Calvary reminds us that this awful inseparableness of sinning and suffering finds its most startling and melting exhibition in the cross of Christ. Even the infinite love of God must needs bow to the inviolability of this law if man is to be saved! This plunges the mind into a mystery too deep for finite understandings to fathom; yet we can at least grasp that somehow the cross of Christ was a Divine necessity.

Yes, sinning and suffering go together. This law operates in the lives of individuals, in the history of nations, and throughout time, and throughout the universe, and has consequences for eternity.

SUPPLICATION AND SALVATION

We are taking a bit longer than we intended over this fourfold feature of sin, suffering, supplication, salvation, in the incident connected with the brazen serpent; but we cannot leave it without certain brief comments on that second pair of significant spiritual realities which it illustrates, namely, *supplication and salvation*. As sinning and suffering go together, so do supplication and salvation. All the way through Scripture this truth is writ large. Sinful man is not saved by any imagined *self-*

righteousness, by his own supposed "good works," or by any accumulation of religious merit, but by the grace of God (as the *source* of salvation) and the sacrifice of a Sinbearer (as the *means* of salvation). The Scripture doctrine is that salvation is by grace alone on God's part, and by faith alone on man's part (albeit, this faith must be a faith which works by love and shows itself in good works as a *result* of salvation).

Supplication and salvation—that is, salvation for the asking, provided it is the right *kind* of asking, and for *God's* way of salvation. This is what the incident surrounding that brazen serpent teaches. It illustrates that real supplication, of course, implies *repentance*—"We have spoken against the Lord and against thee." And it shows that it must include *confession*—"We have sinned." And it further shows that there must be *faith* in God, faith that He can do what is being asked—"Pray unto the Lord, that He take away the serpents from us."

But the supreme significance of such supplication is its admission that *man is unable to save himself*. That is another of the cardinal emphases throughout Holy Scripture. It is a "rock of offence" on which many a proud human heart has defiantly dashed itself, and a "stone of stumbling" to many another whose idea has been that man must "work out" his own salvation. Away back in the dawn of human history we find Cain and Abel each bringing an offering to God. Cain brings an offering of the earth's fruits which he has cultivated. Abel brings a sacrificial lamb. And from that day to this there have been the two sorts of religion in the world—the religion of human culture (the Cain religion), and the religion of Divine redemption (the Abel religion). God rejected and still rejects the offering of Cain. Man is a sinner both legally and morally, both by transgression (what he *does*) and by condition (what he *is*). He is guilty before the law of God, and corrupt in his own nature. He can neither offer an atonement to cover his guilt nor save himself from his own corruption. The Cain religion still leaves Cain a murderer. Man cannot redeem man. Self cannot change self. What we all have to learn first is that if we are to *be* saved it must be by the way which God Himself provides; and this is the way which is illustrated in this episode of the brazen serpent.

Thus far, we are only looking at the *circumference* of the incident, so to speak; and we must reserve a detailed examination of the uplifted serpent itself until our next study. Yet even here, in this union of supplication and salvation, we see at once the great, outstanding, double-feature in God's way of salvation. In response to the people's supplication through Moses, God instructed that an imitation snake must be prominently hoisted so as to be visible throughout that vast, mobile camp of over two million people. The bitten ones were to look to it, and in doing so were to find healing from the death-sting of the infesting serpents. Their salvation thus had both an *objective* and a *subjective* aspect. They were to look for salvation to something altogether *outside* of themselves, even that upraised serpent of brass; but they were also to experience something just as real *within* themselves, even a new life-power setting them free from "the law of sin and death."

That uplifted serpent is (in type) the Christ of the Cross. The power which inwardly cured the venom-inoculated Israelites is (in type) the renewing power of the Holy Spirit. In that uplifted serpent of brass God was showing them (as we shall presently amplify) how He had passed judgment on their sin. Their "looking" to it was an education in faith, and a type of that simple heart-trust on the Lord Jesus Christ which now brings regeneration.

Of course, there was mystery about it. Why or how a "look" to that strange-seeming objective figure should or could effect subjective healing from the viper virus was a mystery which neither priests nor elders could expound. It was something definitely supernatural (as all true conversion to Christ is to-day). It was beyond human explanation. But the mystery of it did not interfere with the reality of it. The vital fact was that *it worked*! All who looked were *saved*!

And that is the vital fact, so far as we ourselves are concerned, about the cross of Christ. It really saves! Or, rather, *HE* saves, the Christ of Calvary. The salvation which comes to us through Him has both its objective and subjective aspects. On that Cross, objectively, Divine judgment was passed upon human sin, atonement was made, and a righteous basis was thereby constituted on which a holy God could righteously pardon all who truly "repent and believe." But, as well as this, by that Cross and from that Christ there flows into the believing soul a new spiritual life—"the Spirit of life in Christ Jesus" (Rom. viii. 2).

Mystery? Yes, fathomless and infinite; but the mystery of it in no way detracts from the saving reality of it on the human side. Profundity? Yes, the Divine philosophy of the Atonement out-matches the intellects of men and angels; yet over against the profundity of its philosophy is the simplicity of its appropriation—"He that *believeth* on the Son *hath* everlasting life" (John iii. 36), of which the type in Numbers xxi is, "Every one that is bitten, when he *looketh* upon it, shall *live*." Oh, this wonderful union of mystery and reality, of profundity and simplicity, in God's way of salvation!

> 'Tis *mystery* all! The Immortal dies!
> Who can explore His strange design?
> In vain the first-born seraph tries
> To sound the depths of love Divine.
> 'Tis *mercy* all, immense and free;
> For, O my God, it found out me!

Years ago, in an American city, the noted infidel, Ingersoll, was advertised to give a lecture on, "The Foundations of the Christian Faith," when he received a remarkable letter from a former schoolmate who lived in the same city. This schoolmate had started out with good promise upon a legal career, had married a beautiful woman, and become the father of two bonny children; but later he had come under the power of drink, and had been dragged down so low that he had lost his good name, his character, his friends, and even his home, breaking his wife's heart, and turning his children into the street. One night a Christian slum-worker found him helplessly drunk in an alley, and took him to a home where he was washed, fed, given hospitality, and told of a Saviour who could save him to the uttermost. By the grace of God and the power of the Cross this human wreck was transformed into a sober and godly man. He rebuilt his shattered home, brought back his children, restored the joys of happy married life to his wife, and attained again to respectability in his calling. Seeing the advertisement of Ingersoll's lecture, he wrote the following letter to the infidel:

"My dear Old Friend,

"I see that to-night you are to deliver a lecture against Christianity and the Bible. Perhaps you know some of my history since we parted, how I disgraced my home and family, lost my character, and all that a man can hold dear in this world. You may know that I went down and down until I was a poor, despised outcast; and when I thought there was none to help and none to save, there came one in the name of Jesus, who told me of His power to help, of His loving-kindness and His tender sympathy; and through the story of the cross of Christ I turned to Him. I brought my wife back to my home, and gathered my children together again, and we are happy now, and I am doing what good I can.

"And now, old friend, would you stand to-night before the people of Pittsburg, and tell them what you have to say against the religion that will come down to the lowest depths of hell and find me, and help me up, and make my life happy, and clothe my children, and give me back home and friends—will you tell them what you have to say against a religion like that?"

Mr. Ingersoll read that letter before his audience, and then said: "Ladies and Gentlemen, I have nothing to say against a religion that will do this for a man. I am here to talk about a religion that is being preached by the preachers. You can find fault with the Church; but there stands One, supreme, and no man has ever dared to point his finger at the character of Christ and find fault with Him."

Yes, it works! The Cross really saves! Our Saviour is able to "save to the uttermost" all who come unto God by Him. As the old Sankey hymn says, "There is life for a look!" Thank God, it is true!—there is "life everlasting" for a look of penitence and faith to the crucified Lord Jesus!

THE TYPE INTERPRETED

What is the real winning of a soul for God? So far as this is done by instrumentality, what are the processes by which a soul is led to God and to salvation? I take it that one of its main operations consists in *instructing* a man that he may know the truth of God. Instruction by the Gospel is the commencement of all real work upon men's minds. Teaching begins the work, and crowns it too. . . . Hence, if we do not teach men something, we may shout, *"Believe! Believe! Believe!"* but what are they to believe? Each exhortation requires a corresponding instruction, or it will mean nothing. *"Escape!"* From what? *"Fly!"* But whither? *"Be converted!"* But what is it to be converted? By what power can we be converted? What from? What to? It is ours, as the Lord's instruments, to make men so to know the truth that they may believe it, and feel its power.

C. H. Spurgeon

THE TYPE INTERPRETED

"And as Moses lifted up the serpent in the wilderness, even so must the Son of Man be lifted up; that whosoever believeth in Him should not perish, but have eternal life."—John iii. 14, 15.

So, THEN, that uplifted serpent of brass preached the Gospel in advance. We have already reflected on this in broad aspect; but now let us examine it more particularly, and we shall find how eloquent that strange-looking remedy was. It was God's answer to a deadly and desperate situation, even as the cross of Christ is, in an infinitely vaster sense. In that old-time camp of Israel men were stricken, suffering, perishing, and "much people of Israel died." To-day men are sin-stricken and suffering and perishing everywhere around us. That brazen serpent of long ago tells us what "Christ crucified" means to perishing sinners to-day.

To begin with, notice *where* that brazen serpent was. Was it inside the Tabernacle? No. Was it among the tents of the priests? No. Was it in the charge of the Levites? No. Now to say the least, that is rather remarkable. Was not that miracle-working metal serpent ordained of God? Had it not therefore a special religious connection? Ought it not then to have been erected inside the precincts of the Tabernacle, where the altar of sacrifice and the brazen laver and the other objective ordinances of Israel's religion were? Well, perhaps we ourselves might have expected to find it so. Perhaps Moses himself at first would expect it to be ordered so. But no; it was *not* to be put inside the Tabernacle. It was to be hoisted high on a pole *outside* the Tabernacle. Salvation by this serpent of brass was outside the Tabernacle, and apart from all ordinances, sacrifices, and priestly ministrations.

Yes, this is striking, right at the outset, and its significance is at once obvious. As it was with the salvation which came through

161

that uplifted serpent, so is it with the Gospel of Christ. Salvation is not by priests, confessionals, communions, or church ceremonials of any kind at all. In that Hebrew camp of long ago, it was not Aaron the priest who had to erect the serpent on the pole, but Moses the layman (for, remember, Moses was not of the Aaronic order, and was therefore simply a "layman"). Similarly, our Lord Jesus Himself, according to Jewish law, was a layman, for He was neither of the family of Aaron nor of the tribe of Levi. He preached in the Temple court, but never ministered at the brazen altar, nor would the Temple authorities have allowed Him to do so for a moment. The apostles also were laymen. Our Lord and the apostles never pointed men to the Temple or to the sacrifices or to the other ordinances, for their salvation. They pointed men to Calvary, which was altogether apart from the Temple and its priests and its ordinances.

But were not the Tabernacle (and later the Temple) and the priesthood and the ordinances of Divine origin and authority? Yes, they were, but their function lay in a different line altogether from that of curing snake-poisoned, fever-racked, dying men and women. They had many comforts and benedictions to bestow on those persons who, having been *already healed* by means of the brazen serpent, now came to offer grateful sacrifices at the Tabernacle altar; but they had no power whatever to *cure* men and women of the fatal sting. Nay, on the contrary (in the absence of any contradicting evidence) it is to be presumed that some among the priests and Levites themselves were bitten and dying, or were perhaps even dead. The point is, that the Tabernacle (as also the Temple later) was the appointed means of access to God and to covenant blessings for those who were *already* in covenant relationship, and who were already healed of the serpent venom. So long as any man was racked with the poison fever, or was in any way infected, he was disqualified from the Tabernacle altogether, for he would have defiled it. Even so, properly understood, the "means of grace" in our sanctuaries to-day are for those who have *been* healed, cleansed, saved, and made meet for communion with God through Christ the Saviour. Sinners must come to Calvary for pardon and cleansing and healing and spiritual renewal *before* they can become true worshippers in the sanctuary, or partakers of "the inheritance of the saints in light."

One of the leading doctrines of the Roman Catholics is that there is "no salvation outside of the Church." By the Church, of course, they mean exclusively *their* church, which fact is enough in itself to make their slogan absurd to those of us outside the Roman church who know something of its record, and read the New Testament for ourselves, and experience the saving reality of the Lord Jesus in our hearts. But even supposing that by "the Church" we were to mean the whole organised church of Christendom, or even the true, spiritual Church consisting of the truly redeemed in Christ, is it true even then that there is "no salvation outside the Church"? Is not the real truth that, in the primary Gospel sense of that word "salvation," *all* salvation is *necessarily* outside the Church? All who become saved necessarily become saved outside the Church, as guilty, hell-deserving sinners. It is by this becoming saved outside the Church—saved by accepting Christ, not by accepting the Church—that souls are *brought into* the Church. Instead of "no salvation outside the Church," the real truth is that *by* salvation we *enter* the true Church!

Yes, it is by penitently and believingly and simple-heartedly accepting Christ as our Saviour, and thus receiving a blood-bought pardon, and cleansing from sin, and a new spiritual nature begotten in us by the regenerating Spirit of God, that we become "saved" in the primary sense of that word, and thus become living members of the true, spiritual Church. What! "No salvation outside the Church"? What needs making plain is that there is no salvation *in* the Church, except in the sense that all who are in it (the true Church) are saved because they are first of all in Christ. Salvation is in Christ, not in the Church. And to be in Christ is to be in the true Church.

Of course, if it be said that only those who are in the true Church are saved, and that in *that* sense there is "no salvation outside the Church," well, that is a very different thing. What we earnestly desire to make emphatic here, however, is that the salvation of the soul does not come by looking to the Church, or to *any* church or system, or to priests, ministers, sacraments,

ordinances, or anything ecclesiastical whatever. The salvation
of perishing sinners is in the uplifted Christ of Calvary, and in
Him alone.

Oh, to make this so clear that none of us will ever doubt it
again or be hazy about it in speaking to others! Look back again
at that serpent of brass in Numbers xxi. No sanctuary curtains
or drapings enfold it or obscure it from view. It is not planted
even in the spacious "outer court" of the Tabernacle. It is *right
outside*, high-hoisted where all may see it. When an Israelite
man or woman was bitten by one of the venomous pests there
was no healing value in a consultation with one of the elders,
or in secretly confessing delinquencies to one of the priests, or in
getting a prescription from one of the camp apothecaries, or in
appearing at the "gate" of the Tabernacle with some expensive
offering. The direction which God gave to Moses was short, clear,
easy: the people must simply look to the serpent on that tall
standard.

And it is well also to observe that although the brazen serpent
was outside the Tabernacle, it was *not* outside the *camp*! That
is where many people to-day seem to think it ought to have been!
But no, there was no need for pilgrimaging away to the outskirts
of the wide-spreading encampment, or dragging weary limbs and
fevered bodies to some sacred spot at a distance beyond. Nor
was the wonder-working, snake-shaped metal ordered to be kept
away from the vulgar gaze by being deposited inside the tent
of one of the leaders well-known for his mystic piety. Nor is
salvation to-day to be found in going outside the camp, in with-
drawing from the dwellings of men to the cloisters of sequestered
monasteries, or in pilgrimaging to sacred shrines, or in following
the dicta of certain teachers or preachers who are supposed to
be special authorities, or in attaching oneself to some pietistic
little sect or clique or idea which is supposed to have the secret
of salvation seclusively in its own little tent! No; there is nothing
seclusionist about God's way of salvation. To all sin-sick, con-
science-stricken, heart-weary, troubled, seeking souls, we say in
God's name and on the authority of His inspired word, "Look
to Jesus only! Look to Jesus uplifted on the Cross! The mystery
of that Cross may be fathomless; the meaning of it may be

profound; but the message of it to you and me is clear and plain and public and gracious and simple—"He that believeth on the Son hath eternal life"! Yes, there uplifted, before the gaze of all, is that wondrous Cross on which the Prince of Glory died. "For God so loved the *world* that He gave His only-begotten Son, that *whosoever* believeth in Him should not perish, but have everlasting life."

But now let us look a bit more closely at the special characteristics of this brazen serpent. There are three features which draw our immediate attention—(1) its appointment; (2) its all-sufficiency; (3) its appropriation.

THE APPOINTMENT OF IT

The first thing which we notice is that this singular form of remedy was *prescribed by God Himself*. It was no invention of Moses, nor the outcome of any suggestion made by Aaron. The word runs, "And JEHOVAH said unto Moses . . ." Moses simply did as he was directed of God. Thus does the serpent of brass at once testify concerning the cross of Christ. The Cross is the God-appointed way of man's salvation. Let the world's wiseacres think or say what they may, it still remains that the Cross is the Divinely chosen means of salvation from sin, both here and hereafter. Self-righteous persons may resent it. Bigoted religionists may resist it. Impenitent sinners may refuse it. Hypocritical formalists may revile it. Prejudiced unbelievers may reject it. But there it is, "towering o'er the wrecks of time," erected by a mightier hand than that of Moses, the heaven-provided standard of deliverance for all who will "look" to it with the eye of faith. As Paul says, in Romans iii. 25, "GOD hath set forth Christ to be a propitiation."

But secondly, that serpent of brass was remarkably *informing*. In Old Testament typology the serpent is the symbol or type of sin, and brass of Divine judgment. Therefore, a "serpent," cast in "brass," and then raised high up on a "pole," was manifestly intended to display the fact of Divine judgment on sin. God had now passed judgment on the people's sin, and deliverance was being wrought. Correspondingly, that is what we see at

Calvary, Divine judgment on human sin. Not that the Father punished His sinless Son (which would be a revulsive doctrine), but that He there passed righteous and necessary judgment on sin, and the incarnate Son, as man's sinless Representative, voluntarily bore it in our stead. Yes, in that wondrous Cross I see sin judged—the world's sin and my own sin; and I know that if I rest by faith on the great Sin-bearer, I can never perish, because He utterly exhausted sin's penalty. That serpent of brass to which the old-time Israelites had to look was, by Divine direction, a *"fiery* serpent," reminding the beholders at once of the "fiery serpents" which swarmed the camp. Yet it was a fiery serpent riveted through the head or staked through the body, and publicly exhibited as stingless and dead! Even so, when I look upon the Christ of Calvary, although I see sin in all its fieriness and burning pangs being endured by my dear Lord, my sinless, substitutionary Expiator, I also see the ugly reptile, sin, publicly exhibited as now helpless and dead. Its power over me is broken! The "Seed of the woman" has "broken the head of the serpent"! The sting is taken even out of death, for "the sting of death is sin." And although fiery serpents still infest the camp, although I am still tempted by "the world and the flesh and the devil," there is a saving and healing virtue now and for evermore in that wonderful, wonderful Cross!

This leads to a third reflection on that Divinely appointed serpent of brass. It was the *only* remedy. God's plan was not that some should be saved one way and some another. They were all victims of the one fell plague, and they were all to find their cure in the one and only prescribed antidote. I wonder if some of those who flattered themselves as being the aristocracy or upper stratum of Israelitish society took offence at having to do just the same thing as the basest and poorest of the multitude? I wonder if some of the intellectuals, inflated by an extra imbibing of Egyptian "learning," thought there ought to be some more cultured or recondite formula of healing for themselves than for their more rustic comrades? I do not know; but I do know this, that whatever their thoughts may have been, there was in actual fact only the one way of salvation. And I

have a feeling, too, that whatever they may have been socially
or intellectually, or in any other way, when once they really
felt the fire and fever of the serpent-venom burning their veins
and sickening their heads, they were all equally glad to get into
the open and look to that precious remedy, shining in the bright
rays of the Eastern sun.   Oh, how we need to insist on the cross
of Christ to-day as the *only* real remedy for human sin! We are
living in days of multiplied false panaceas. Men and women look
to them with pathetic eagerness, only to suffer a recoil of frus-
tration and deeper helplessness.   Listen, O ye sin-sick sons of
men, to the word of God: "There is NONE OTHER NAME
UNDER HEAVEN given among men, whereby we must be
saved."

We see yet another truth illustrated in that uplifted serpent.
It was a serpent of "brass," and therefore it was an *enduring*
remedy. Had it been of clay or wood or some other substance
less durable than metal, not only would it have been without
the fiery reflection which it was meant to have, but it would
not have survived the intense heat of the Eastern sun. At all
events, it *was* of "brass," so it lasted on and on. In fact we
read of it seven hundred years later, in the reign of Judah's king,
Hezekiah. It is even so with the cross of Christ. While there
is an absolute finality in the Cross as an act of atonement, there
is a ceaseless continuity of efficacy in it, and an infinite wealth
of pardoning grace released by it, and an endless stream of
healing virtue flowing from it.

And yet once more we note that the serpent of brass was
intendedly *conspicuous*. By Divine instruction it was erected
high upon a pole in the middle of the camp, for all to see. The
Book of Numbers gives Israel's man-power at that time (from
twenty years upward) as 603,550, plus the Levites, 22,300. On
the basis of this adult male census, scholars compute the whole
nation as over two million. These were mobilised in quadrangular
formation, making a vast, movable camp which would be about
twelve miles round. It may be wondered, therefore, how the
uplifted brazen serpent could be seen by all the people in that
large area. Some of the tents of Issachar and Naphtali may
have been over a mile and a half away from it. Well, there is

not a hint that anyone had difficulty in that connection. The pole would be much higher than the artists' pictures of it which one usually sees, and if there was a knoll or hillock anywhere near, it would be planted thereon for extra prominence. Travellers in that part tell us that the air is so translucent there that such an object could be seen for miles in any direction. All were *intended* to see it; and all were *enabled* to see it. So is it with the cross of Christ. There it stands in mid-history. For the majority of the human race it divides all history into B.C. and A.D. The message of its redeeming significance was preached throughout the Roman world of old, and is being carried through all five continents to-day. But let us come right to our own hearts; we ourselves *can* see it clearly enough if we *will*. The Holy Scriptures lift it up to us, for it is the supreme subject of their inspired pages. The Holy Spirit also makes it conspicuous to our inward eye, if we will let Him. Thousands of churches and sermons and books and tracts also still uplift that Cross as indeed the sinner's never-failing refuge. Oh, that we might even now persuade some unsaved one to "look away to Jesus"!

THE ALL-SUFFICIENCY OF IT

But now consider briefly the second inclusive feature pertaining to that serpent of brass, namely, its all-sufficiency. As we have said, it was the *only* remedy, but, thank God, *no other was needed*. The last bit of the narrative says: "It came to pass that if a serpent had bitten any man, when he beheld the serpent of brass, he lived." Note the following aspects of this all-sufficiency.

First, the remedy availed *wherever a person was bitten*. The prophet Isaiah speaks of "fiery flying serpents." The reference is to their trick of contracting themselves and then springing upwards. Thus, a man might be bitten not only in the feet but in the higher parts of the body. Or perhaps a man might be gathering sticks and suddenly feel the fangs of one of these uncoiling snakes in his hand or arm. But it mattered not where the wound was: a look to the uplifted miracle-worker brought perfect cure. Even so is there provision for all manner of sin

in the uplifted Christ of Calvary. Sin victimises different people
in different ways. It takes varying forms in varying natures.
But in whichever way it poisons and pollutes, whether its wounds
are polite or vulgar, whether its virus is more mental than sensual
or more sensual than mental, there is healing and cleansing,
pardon and power in the Cross.

> There's a place where the sin-sick find healing,
>   And where hearts are washed whiter than snow;
> Where forgiveness comes tenderly stealing,
>   And the contrite find heaven below.
> There's a place where a wonderful shining
>   Floods our lives with new meaning and light;
> Where we rise from the gloom of repining
>   With new purpose and gladness and might!

But the remedy was also all-sufficient in the sense that it
availed *however serious a person's condition*. No doubt, most who
got bitten would look without delay to the high-hoisted snake of
brass, flashing in the golden rays of the noon, or darkly silhouetted
against the bright blue of the sky, or reflecting the crimson of a
rich sunset; but perhaps there were others who, for one reason
or another, procrastinated. There are some serpent bites which
for the moment cause little or no bleeding or swelling or sensation, and the bitten person thinks the puncture must have been
harmless. Then, presently, as the arteries are affected, a critical
condition suddenly develops. Or perhaps some who were bitten
were of dim vision and had to be conducted to the immediate
vicinity of the cure, getting quickly worse all the way. Or
perhaps, with youthful bravado, some strapping young Hebrew
would say, "Oh, *I* shall come to no harm from *that* couple of
pin-pricks in my wrist! Why, they are nothing compared with
the slashes I have had in skirmishes with bandits! And even if
there *is* a trickle of poison in my system, I can soon throw it
off!" Yes, it may possibly be that here and there some such
over-confident youth may thus have spoken, only to find ere
long, however, not only maddening fever, but paralysis, and
blurring of the eyes. Still, it mattered not how far gone a person's

condition, if there were but the strength left to turn a languid eye to the serpent of brass, there was complete restoration. How truly, in this respect also, does the brazen serpent prefigure the Cross of Calvary! It matters not how blackened by guilt a soul may be; that miracle-fount washes "whiter than snow." It matters not how poisoned by sin the mind may be, or how agued by passions the heart may be, that wonderful remedy can cleanse and heal and renew.

Again, that brazen serpent was all-sufficient inasmuch as it availed *however many times a person might be bitten.* It would have been a poor look-out for most of the people if it had only worked once for each person, for the serpent pests lurked everywhere. It is not improbable that some of the people may have been bitten a score of times. Again and again unwary individuals would be taken by surprise, and start back with a cry of pain, just too late to avoid the swift fangs of those springy reptiles; but almost as soon as they felt the first sensation or spasm which betokened the deadly saliva in their veins, they would gratefully glance away to the ever-efficacious effigy upraised for their cure. And the more often they put it to the proof, so the more precious it would become to them. A multitude beyond number could give glad testimony that it is equally so with the cross of Christ. When we accept Him as our Saviour, our sins are "forgiven us for His name's sake" (1 John ii. 12), we have "peace with God through our Lord Jesus Christ" (Rom. v. 1) our guilt is completely cancelled (Rom. viii. 1), and the Holy Spirit quickens us into new spiritual life (Eph. ii. 5; Rom. viii. 2). In a word, we become saved, in the sense of immediate forgiveness, reconciliation, and justification. But does God thereupon take us immediately away from this sinful earth to His sinless heaven? Or does He see to it that henceforth sin never attacks us again? No; we still remain in the world, and the world still remains infested with the serpents of sin. Moreover, the serpents of sin seem, if possible, more insidious and troublesome than ever. Over against the keener eye which God has given us, they seem determined to trick us by still cleverer ambush and camouflage. But if through unwariness we fall victim to the noisome pestilence, do we thereby become unsaved and "lost" again? A thousand times, "No"! Thank God, there is perpetual efficacy in the Cross! It *keeps on* providing forgiveness and cleansing and healing and renewal and fellowship with God.

Still further, the brazen serpent was all-sufficient in that it equally availed *whoever the bitten person was*. There were no discriminations. There were no degrees or variations in its applicability. Old or young, priest or Levite, prince or peasant, elder or underling, owner or slave, good or bad, religious or irreligious, pedigree Israelite or proselyte of the "mixed multitude" who had come up with Israel out of Egypt and reared children in the wilderness—it made no difference so far as the freeness and potency of the God-appointed cure were concerned. Even the kind of life lived beforehand was not allowed either to give preference or to be a disqualification. No account was taken of a person's respectability, or regularity of devotions, or the number of sacrifices offered at the Tabernacle, or of the charities dispensed, or of confessions made. And so is it with the salvation of the soul to-day. The offer of God in the Gospel overrides all distinctions of race and colour, caste and class, upbringing and education. It embraces all human beings indiscriminately in its magnanimous idiom, "WHOSOEVER." It equally avails for all; and Jesus says, "Him that cometh to Me I will in no wise cast out."

> Jesus never answered "Nay,"
>   When a sinner sought His aid;
> Jesus never turned away
>   When request to Him was made.
> No, each weary, needy one
> Found a Friend in God's dear Son.

What was true then is true now. The best and the worst, the highest and the lowest, may come and find salvation in the dear Saviour. When those plagued Hebrews of long ago felt the serpent-fire inflaming their blood, they never thought of boasting their pedigree, upbringing, social status, respectability, or anything else. They knew they were victims and that they were sure to die unless the uplifted serpent of brass healed them. Their one question was: "Does it avail for *me*?" And soon, all

who "looked" were able to give grateful testimony, "Yes, it
does avail for me! It is the power of God unto salvation to every
one that looketh." So is it with the Christ of Calvary—

> His blood can make the foulest clean;
> His blood avails for *me*!

Just once more, that serpent of brass was all-sufficient, also,
in the sense that it was absolutely *infallible*. There is not a case
on record, nor even the faintest, accidental hint, of any man,
woman or child among all the thousands of Israel, ever looking
to that serpent-topped pillar and finding it uncertain or unavail-
ing. If it *had* failed in any instance there would have been some
big reason for it, and the fact would certainly have been written
down for our learning. But no; it worked infallibly—*infallibly*.
And from the day that the dying felon looked to Jesus on that
middle cross of the three, right down to this present moment,
never has a soul really looked in simple faith to the Lord Jesus
for salvation and found *Him* to fail. He is the *infallible* Saviour.
The vilest of the vile, the poorest of the poor, the weakest of
the weak, the most hopeless of the hopeless, the guiltiest of the
guilty, and the most enslaved of all the devil's slaves have found
Jesus to be the infallible Saviour. When certificates of supposed
cure from inebriety have proved not worth the paper they were
written on, Jesus has completely liberated abject drunkards.
When psychology and psychiatry have proved worse than
useless, Jesus has wrought the miracle of deliverance and
transformation.

> There's a place where life's failures are mended,
>   Where frustration and helplessness cease;
> There's a place where sin's bondage is ended,
>   And the captive leaps forth in release.
> There's a place where life's woundings and scourgings
>   Are healed by a heavenly balm,
> Where our fearings and tossings and surgings
>   Are stilled into wonderful calm.

There's a place where life's storm clouds are parted,
  And the glory of heaven breaks through;
Where the tear-dimmed and long broken-hearted
  Find the strength to begin life anew.
There's a place where the shackles are broken,
  Where the prisoners of sin are set free,
Where the word of forgiveness is spoken,
  And the place is called *CALVARY*!

To every sin-sick, guilt-burdened, habit-enslaved sinner we say again, "Look to Jesus! He is mighty to save!" His death is the atonement for your sin. His precious blood can cleanse away all your black record, so that it will not be remembered against you any more for ever. His Cross is your peace with God. His living power is your hope of liberation from the bonds that bind you; for, remember, the Christ of the Cross is the One who conquered death and lives in triumph over the grave. Certainly it is to the Cross that you must look, for it was thereon that the great atoning sacrifice was offered once for all; yet it is to a *living* Christ also that you must look, for it is He who now makes the *power* of His Cross *real* in the lives of men and women who accept Him. To all who simply and sincerely trust Him He is the infallible Saviour.

THE APPROPRIATION OF IT

And now, finally, observe how illuminatingly the *appropriation* of healing through the brazen serpent illustrates the receiving of salvation through the cross of Christ. God said to Moses: "Make thee a fiery serpent, and set it upon a pole; and it shall come to pass that every one that is bitten, *when he LOOKETH upon it*, shall live."

In this connection, the first thing we note is that the appropriation of the remedy was *easy*. All a man had to do for healing was to "look." He did not have to pay for it. He did not have to work for it. He did not have to earn it. He did not have to merit it. He did not have to wait for it. He did not even have to pray for it. All he had to do was to accept it. He did not have to undergo a course of preparatory religious instruction. He did not have to consult a priest or an elder or even Moses himself. All he had to do was to "look" to the appointed standard. Certainly, nothing could have been simpler or easier than *that*! So is it as regards the receiving of salvation through the Lord Jesus Christ. The Gospel assurance runs, "Believe on the Lord Jesus Christ, and thou shalt be saved." "He that believeth on the Son hath everlasting life." Salvation comes through our simply believing: and believing on the Lord Jesus is really just as simple, in a spiritual sense, as looking to that brazen serpent was, in a physical sense. What a "look" is to the eye of the body, saving faith is to the eye of the heart. Would we know Jesus as our personal Saviour?—then let us forever banish from our minds the idea that saving faith toward Him is something mysterious or complicated, or something possible only to the intellectual. Why, obviously, it is not the faith itself which saves us, but the One toward whom we exercise it. We must not make faith itself the Saviour! CHRIST is the Saviour. Therefore, the fact is that the simpler and more child-like our faith is, the better.

> Oh, how unlike the complex works of man,
> Heaven's easy, artless, unencumbered plan!
> No meretricious graces to beguile,
> No clustering ornaments to clog the pile:
> From ostentation as from weakness free,
> It stands, like the cerulean arch we see,
> Majestic in its own simplicity.
> Inscribed above the portal, from afar
> Conspicuous, as the brightness of a star,
> Legible only by the light they give,
> Stand the soul-quickening words—BELIEVE
>   AND LIVE!

Of course, when the Israelites were first told that healing was to come simply through a "look," many of them would think that such a way of cure seemed highly *improbable*. Some of them would say, either inwardly or outwardly, "What! healed

just by a 'look' at that snake-shaped thing suspended up there?"
That is how people think or speak to-day about God's way of
salvation for us. Only a short time ago, we heard a really bur-
dened enquirer say, "Somehow, this being saved just through
'believing' seems too simple to be real." Strange irony!—people
seem as though they can "believe" that salvation comes almost
any other way than *by* "believing"! If only they can *do* something, or *give* something, or get some emotional "experience,"
then (they think) they are on the right "tack." Well, however
improbable healing by a "look" may have seemed to the Israelites,
all who tried it found it to be the one way which really cured
them. And however improbable salvation by simple trust on the
Lord Jesus may seem to some people to-day, all who *do* simple-
heartedly believe upon Him are saved—because His atoning work
on Calvary was full and final and for ever.

Again, that "look" which God made the means of healing
among the Israelite viper-victims was intendedly and instruc-
tively *humbling*. They might have been told to look at the golden
figure of a cherub, or at some beautiful object of nature; and
God could just as easily have conveyed healing to them thereby.
But no, it was a serpent, an ugly serpent, at which they were to
look; and every "look" would at once remind them of their own
sin and of the hateful serpents cursing the camp! So is it with
the Cross of our dear Saviour. That very Cross which saves us
brings home to us as nothing else ever could the real ugliness
of our sin. The *uttermost* ugliness of sin is seen, not in its violating
of God's holy law, but in its nailing the sinless, harmless, beautiful,
loving Son of God in shame and mockery and gloating cruelty
to that ignominious Cross. No man can look at that Cross, and
take salvation proudly. It convicts us. It humbles us. It melts
our hard hearts. It makes us know what sinners indeed we are.
Although we ourselves were not born when Jesus hung there,
we were present in the foreknowledge of God; and by our sins
we were implicated in that awful act of repudiation; for that
event on Calvary was representative, both retrospectively and
anticipatively. The whole human race was in it. It was human
sin which did it; and a part of that sin was *ours*. We may not
be able to sound the depthless mystery of it, but somehow the

sin of each individual member of the human race added conscious weight to the sufferings of the sinless Sinbearer. *My* sins
somehow added consciously to the expiatory sufferings of God's
dear Son! *My* sins helped to weave that crown of thorns! O
Sin, thou art never so ugly as when I see thee nailing the meek
and lowly Jesus to that Cross! O soul of mine, thou canst never
behold Jesus hanging there and not hate sin! Terrible Cross!
Wonderful Saviour! Truly, there is nothing like a sight of Calvary
to melt us down in humility and contrition.

Still further, we note that the appropriation of the remedy by
those serpent-plagued Hebrews was *individual*. Each one must
look for himself or herself alone. None could look for another.
There was no getting healed by proxy. Dying sons and daughters
were not cured because godly fathers and mothers had proved
the reality of the salvation before them. No one could help
another except by doing what Moses himself was doing, namely,
urging the perishing ones to look to God's remedy, displayed
high aloft. The old proverb is true enough: "You may lead a
horse to water, but you cannot make him drink." All we can
do for unsaved souls to-day is to tell them the way of salvation,
to explain to them as best we can why the Cross saves, to help
remove their doubts and difficulties, to invite them, urge them,
pray for them, point them: but we cannot *make* them believe,
and we cannot believe *for* them. No, for although the word
"whosoever" means all, it also means *each*; and each must
believe for himself or herself alone. In every conversion, our
Saviour's word to the trusting soul is, "*Thy* faith hath made
thee whole; go in peace and be whole of thy plague" (Mark v. 34).

Lastly, we observe that the cure which came by looking to
that brazen serpent was *instantaneous*. There is no indication
whatever that any of the cures were gradual or delayed. There
was no need for a convalescent home in the camp! Every case
was a desperate one; for every Israelite who fell casualty was
certain to die quickly of that fatal virus which no human power
could neutralise or nullify. There was not a hypodermic or specific
known to any physician in Israel which could counteract that
deadly spittle in the blood-stream of a viper-victim. But if each
case was desperate, the cure was immediate, by simply a "look"

to the metal serpent fastened to the top of that tall stake! So is it now: every unsaved soul is in desperate peril. "Sin, when it is finished, bringeth forth death" (James i. 15). "The wages of sin is death" (Rom. vi. 23). Sin brings a worse than physical death, a deeper and darker death in the world beyond this present and visible scene. Yet amid this world's scene of sin and death the cross of Christ towers up, and all who look thereto in simple, sincere heart-trust are saved, here and now, saved *instantaneously*! When once we become "saved"—by accepting Christ and being "born again" of the Holy Spirit—then, of course, the living of the Christian life is a progressive *process*; but being "saved," in the sense of accepting Christ, and receiving pardon and cleansing and justification and peaçe with God and promise of heaven, is *not* a process: it is a *CRISIS*, the glad crisis of a moment!—of one, destiny-deciding moment when the heart is opened to receive the once-crucified but now living Saviour. Unsaved one, you may become saved now, this very minute, by simple-heartedly welcoming the Lord Jesus as your very own. Oh, that some unsaved sinner may even now turn the eye of faith to the Divine remedy, and become SAVED!

> Saviour, at last I plainly see
> My urgent, utter need of Thee;
> I who have thought myself too good
> To need a Saviour's cleansing blood.
> Self-righteously I've scorned to own
> I ever feared Thy judgment throne;
> And oft, alas, I've dared to say
> I never would be "saved" this way.
>
> Oh, strange and wilful blindness mine,
> To scorn a saving love like Thine,
> To run the tragic risk and loss
> Of proudly turning from Thy cross!
> But now, O Lord, with burning tears,
> I humbly own my sins and fears;
> Thy Spirit, Lord, has worked within;
> My heart is broken for my sin.

Thy promise, Saviour, tells me how
I may be saved, and know it now;
Thyself hast said, if I "believe"
Salvation I at once receive.
Thy cross a full atonement made,
My sin was borne, the price was paid.
My one and only trust art Thou;
In simplest faith, *I take Thee now*.

FOUR DUAL ASPECTS

There was quoted to my father (the Rev. W. Marsh, D.D.) a saying of old Fuller's—"He that falls into sin is a man. He that grieves at sin is a saint. He that boasts of sin is a devil." My father replied: "Only one thing more: He that *forgives* it is *GOD*."

Miss Marsh

When wounded sore, the stricken soul
  Lies bleeding and unbound,
One only hand, a pierced hand,
  Can salve the sinner's wound.

Lift up that bleeding hand, O Lord,
  Unseal that cleansing tide;
We have no shelter from our sin
  But in Thy wounded side.

C. F. Alexander

FOUR DUAL ASPECTS

IN OUR preceding study we sought to elucidate and apply the principal evangelistic significances latent in the uplifted serpent of brass. Our attention was focused upon the brazen serpent itself rather than upon the historical episode of which it is the arresting centre-point. Let us now reflect again upon its immediate environment, reviewing the incident in total. We shall find here points of pertinent applicability to our own times which may well cause us to pause and ponder. The brief account in Numbers xxi. 4–9 takes little space. Read it through again (see page 136).

We have already pointed out the fourfold contour of the episode —sin, suffering, supplication, salvation; and how these four go in two pairs. This presence of a twofold aspect of things persists significantly right through. The sinning was twofold. The suffering was twofold. The supplication was twofold. The salvation was twofold.

TWOFOLD SIN

Verse 5 says, "And the people spake against God and against Moses: Wherefore have ye brought us up out of Egypt to die in the wilderness? for there is no bread, neither is there any water; and our soul loatheth this light bread." Thus the people rebelled against the way by which God *led* them, and against the food by which God *fed* them. Is not that the outstanding double sin of men to-day? They rebel against God's will as their way, and against God's word as the true food of the soul. The suffering which scourges the world to-day may all be traced to this.

Those old-time grumblers spoke against the *way* by which God led them. We can sympathetically appreciate that "the soul of the people was much discouraged because of the way" (verse 4). They were having to "*compass* the land of Edom" because the Edomites had refused to let them pass through. Yet their outburst was unreasonable. Thirty-eight years before this, God had brought Israel to Kadesh-barnea, to enter the promised land, and the people had unbelievingly refused. Since then they had "marked time," pasturising in the open country. Through all those years God had daily supplied them with "manna," and in time of drought had miraculously given water from the rock (xx. 2–13). He had given abnormal durability to the shoes on their feet and the clothes on their bodies (Deut. viii. 4). All this, despite their rebellious unbelief! And now, the long thirty-eight years hiatus is over. God calls them to "march" again toward Canaan. Yet at the first trial they flare out in defiance!

Men and nations, governments and peoples, are still struggling to bring themselves into some Canaan which they continually promise themselves; but they never attain it, because they will only have it by their own will and in their own way. God's way seems too long or too taxing or too humbling. Meanwhile the goodness of God continues; but the fiery serpents of sin and suffering everywhere scourge the world, so that a great wail ascends to heaven!

And, as we have said, those ungrateful Hebrews also spoke disdainfully of the *food* by which God fed them. They gave the manna an opprobrious epithet, exclaiming, "Our soul loatheth this light bread!" Yet the manna was a daily miracle, food direct from heaven, of which the psalmist, centuries later, sang, "men did eat angels' food." Unquestionably the manna was a diet provided for health's sake in view of the altogether unparalleled exigencies of the wilderness journeyings; and it is notable that no sickness or epidemic occurred all the while that it was the staple diet. Yet here they wickedly stigmatised it!

And what were they but types of a similar attitude in men's hearts to-day? As it was with Christ, the *living* Word from heaven, so is it with the Bible, the *written* word from heaven, it is "despised and rejected of men." See the dishonour heaped upon it during the last hundred years by its pretended friends, the "higher critics"! See how it is rejected to-day in the councils of the nations! See with what avidity men will gulp down the most extravagant fancies of evolutionists rather than grant for a moment, despite the worthiest evidences, that the Bible could possibly be a Divinely inspired revelation! And how men are cursed in consequence!—ever learning, yet never able to come to a knowledge of the truth. Ever seeking peace, yet ever making war! Ever promising themselves Utopia, but rushing headlong to Armageddon! Meanwhile, the fiery serpents of sin and suffering abound; for despite all our advances in medical knowledge and surgical skill, the race's sufferings to-day are more than ever!

Yes, the sin of those old-time Israelites was two-fold—against the way which God led them and the food which God gave them; but it also expressed itself in a two-fold *direction*, for our verse says, "And the people spake against *God* and against *Moses*." Their quarrel was with God first and Moses after. That is ever the sequence of men's sinning and self-inflicted suffering. Man is first of all wrong toward God, and as a result he is forever wrong with his fellow-men. Our leaders wear out their days endeavouring to put man right with man. When we tell them that the only sure way of accomplishing this is first to put men right with God, we are politely ignored or superiorly bowed out as unpractical religious enthusiasts who do not understand the economic or political factors involved.

Yet the truth is, that as soon as a man becomes right with God through conversion to Christ, he begins to readjust all his manward relationships. He becomes a better workman, a better citizen, and a better member of the community in general. Why, every historic revival of Christianity has shown us that such revivals do more to effect economic, political, and social reconciliations in a short spell than years and years of round-table conferences at which God is not honoured. Men in general, however, will not have this. So the trouble goes on. As it was with the twofold sin of those old-time Israelites, so is it to-day, on a vaster scale and under more complex circumstances than ever. Men refuse God's way and God's word. They are wrong toward God; and therefore both the most ambitious and the most desperate expedients of human contriving fail to put men right with each other.

TWOFOLD SUFFERING

Look again now at the suffering which sin brought upon those rebellious tribes as they skirted the land of Edom. Verse 6 says: "And the Lord sent fiery serpents among the people, and they bit the people; and much people of Israel died." Travellers tell us that the area covered by the Israelite "wandering" was dreaded for its snake-infestedness. Why then had the camp known no incursions of these deadly pests before? The people might have known that it was because of an invisible Divine guardianship. But now, as they despise the Divine guidance, they forfeit that protection. Those who will not be Divinely *guided* cannot be Divinely *guarded*. Those who despise the Divine *provision* deprive themselves of the Divine *protection*. The invisible restraint is now withdrawn, the "fiery serpents" swarm in, and soon a heart-rending wail of woe rises to heaven from those thousands of pain-smitten, grief-stricken households. How often it happens that we will only learn the extent of our sin by the extent of our suffering!

Now there are two things which at once impress us concerning the suffering of those serpent-bitten people. First, the effect of the serpent-bites would undoubtedly be acutely *painful*. The malignant reptiles are called "fiery" serpents. This, we believe, referred primarily to their appearance; but presumably it betokened also the fiery effect of their sting. I suppose that as the virus circulated with the blood-stream, such toxemic inflammation would ensue, and eventually such a climax of burning fever consume the system, that every nerve would seem like a strand of flame and every vein a stream of liquid fire. Even so is the effect of *sin* painful. Sometimes sin is directly responsible for suffering in the body. And speaking of the race in total, all bodily suffering is due to man's fall, in Adam, and to the incoming of mortality thereby. But what we are thinking of more particularly here is the suffering which sin inflicts within the *individual*. Oh, the bite of that deadly viper, sin, is painful. "The way of transgressors is hard!" (Prov. xiii. 15). Even where sin does not burn the arteries and temples with literal toxic as in the case of the inebriate and his intoxicating liquors, or gnaw away the

vitals with putred canker as in the case of the venerial wanton,
or distend and inflame the organs, as in the case of the inveterate
glutton, oh, what a fire from hell can sin set burning in the
mind! Ask anyone who has sinned madly and suffered correspondingly, which is the worse, the physical or the mental torture
afterward inflicted! Sin!—the very word begins with the letter
"S," the shape of the writhing serpent; and every time we pro-
nounce the word we seem to hear the hiss!

But there is more to add. Away back in that Israelite camp,
the bite of the serpents, besides being painful, was *fatal*. There
was no human cure. Death was certain. If at the beginning of
the plague there existed any doubt on that score in the people's
minds, it was quickly dispelled, for soon they saw their friends
and relatives lying as corpses everywhere around. So is it with
that moral and spiritual toxemia in human nature which we call
sin. It is a condition of spiritual death leading to a still deeper
and eternal death.

There is a sense in which unsaved sinners are already in a
state of spiritual death. For instance, in Ephesians ii. 4, 5, Paul
writes, "But God, who is rich in mercy, for His great love where-
with He loved us, even when we were *dead in sins*, hath quickened
us together with Christ." Such spiritual death consists in spiritual
darkness of the mind and the non-functioning of that highest
part of our being called the "spirit." Unsaved souls, men and
women who have never washed away their sins in the cleansing
blood of Christ and have never been born again into new spiritual
life by the regenerating Spirit of God, are only finer or coarser
specimens of the same spiritually dead material needing regeneration. Even in this spiritually dead condition, however, moral
response to the Gospel is possible, and "whosoever believeth" is
saved; but to pass in this condition from earth to the vast Beyond
is to go into a yet deeper darkness. In that eternal sphere beyond
this present scene, the Bible speaks of a higher life in which
there is no more death, and of a deeper death in which there is
no more life! That is the death of eternal separation from God.
Oh, how this twofold effect of sin should strike fear into the
minds of all who are foolishly dandling the viper of sin!

TWOFOLD SUPPLICATION

Verse 7 says: "The people came to Moses and said, We have
sinned; for we have spoken against the Lord, and against thee;
Pray unto the Lord, that He take away the serpents from us.
And Moses prayed for the people."

Note here again the two aspects. First there is *confession*:
"We have sinned." What at first had seemed excusable is now
seen to be *sin*: "We have sinned!" And the confession is not
merely general; it is particular: "We have spoken against the
Lord and against thee." Nor was the confession merely formal
or artificial. Besides the sting of the serpents there was now a
genuine sting of conscience. Besides suffering bodies there were
now sorrowing hearts. They were really repenting of their rash
ingratitude and rebellion. One of the most disturbing characteristics of our own times is a prevailing insensitiveness to the
wrongness of sin. There is the lack of the *consciousness* of sin.
The greatest need of our time is not bigger wages, shorter hours,
better conditions, free insurance, financial prosperity, but *godly
repentance*. This is the first step toward real salvation and restoration in the life of any country or community or individual. If
these words of mine now reach the heart of some unsaved soul,
I would say, "Repent, and confess your sin to God. There are
scores of assurances in God's word that He will hear you. Your
sins may have been very black and ugly, as was the case with
those old-time Hebrews. Your heart and life may be as sin-
poisoned as their bodies were snake-poisoned. You may feel
that your condition is hopeless (and so it is apart from Jesus
the Saviour). But if with honest contrition you now confess your
sinning and suffering to God, He will hear you for Jesus' sake,
as certainly as He heard the cry of confession from the lips of
those serpent-bitten Israelites."

But, secondly, besides confession, there was *entreaty*. They
said to Moses: "Pray to the Lord that He take away the serpents
from us." They felt themselves to be such transgressors that
they were unable to pray for themselves; therefore they asked
Moses to pray for them. I myself have seen men and women
like that. They felt too sinful to be able to pray for themselves;

they had to ask some Christian worker to pray *for* them. And sometimes I have knelt before God with a man or woman who simply did not know how to frame a prayer into words, even to ask for pardon and cleansing through the precious blood of the Lord Jesus. Well, if these words of mine reach some despairing sinner who feels too sinful even to pray, my advice is: Go to some Christian believer and say, "Pray for me; pray for salvation to come to me, while I kneel with you." It is notable that the people did not go to Aaron the priest and ask *him* to pray for them. They knew instinctively that it was not just a priest or religion they needed, but a special salvation; and they sensed that salvation must come from God direct, according as Moses His evangelist should announce.

And *did* Moses pray for them? He did. It is written, "And Moses prayed for the people." The very one whom they have so wronged is only too willing to pray for them as he sees their sorrow and suffering. And so is it with those of us who know the Saviour; however much this one or that one may have opposed us or wronged us, yet knowing as we do the terror of a Christless eternity, of the "outer darkness" and the "weeping and wailing and gnashing of teeth," and knowing the graciousness of the Lord, we pray with intense concern for them, especially so when they come to us, sin-burdened, and ask us to do so.

And did God *answer* Moses' prayer for the people? He did! And does He answer prayer for the salvation of souls to-day, in the name of Jesus? He does! Unsaved but now repenting soul, pray now! Entreat God to save you now, through the Saviour's substitutionary death of atonement on your behalf! Jesus says, "Him that cometh unto Me, I will in no wise cast out." Solomon's aphorism in Proverbs xxviii. 13, truly preaches the Gospel in advance—"He that covereth his sins shall not prosper; but whoso confesseth and forsaketh them shall have mercy." And the Gospel promise in 1 John i. 9, runs, "If we confess our sins, He (God) is faithful and just to forgive us our sins, and to cleanse us all from unrighteousness"—all through the precious blood of Christ. Yes, unsaved one, ask God now to save you; and if it will help you, get some Christian brother or sister to pray with you. The God who heard long ago will hear you also, and will save you for Jesus' sake.

TWOFOLD SALVATION

God's word to Moses was: "Make thee a fiery serpent and set it upon a pole; and it shall come to pass that everyone that is bitten, when he looketh upon it shall live." Clearly, then, as the sinning and the suffering and the supplication were twofold, so was the salvation. It was both objective and subjective. They were to look to something *outside* of themselves, yet at the same time they were to experience something *inside* of themselves. It is the very same in the salvation of the soul. It is both objective and subjective. We are to look to something outside ourselves, and at the same time there is a wonderful change takes place within us.

We are to look in simple faith to the Cross of Calvary. When Jesus hung on that Cross He did something which we could never have done for ourselves, and He did it once for all, so that it never needs doing again. With an infinite fulness and an absolute finality He made atonement for the sin of man. No mere creature, however high in the ranks of being, could have done that; for all creatures are God's property, and have nothing independently of their own which they could offer as a satisfaction over against human guilt. Moreover, even the highest of created beings is still only finite, and therefore utterly incapable of consciously expiating human sin.

But the Lord Jesus Christ, although *really* man, is not *merely* man. He is the eternal Son of God, having now also taken to Himself our human nature, in the mystery of His incarnation. Because He is really man He represents me to God. Because He is also God He represents God to me. He is the Middleman, or "Mediator." In Him, at Calvary, God and man meet judicially on the awful issue of sin. Because Christ is not only man but the *sinless* Man, He represents man acceptably. Because He is not merely a creature but the eternal Son of God, He is able to *exhaust* in His infinite being the penalty due to human sin in all its vast totality. Freely and fully and finally He made atonement. He hung there voluntarily and vicariously and victoriously. Mark those three V's. He did it *voluntarily*—of His own free choice because He loved us. He did it *vicariously*—in our place and as our substitute. He did it *victoriously*—over sin and Satan, for He "bore away the sin of the world," and made deliverance possible for all the serpent's victims!

We are to look to Him, the Christ of Calvary, as the serpent-bitten Israelites were to look to the brazen serpent on the pole. It is no use looking to anything inside ourselves, to our supposedly strong will, to our religious sympathies, to our repentance and desire for salvation—imagining that these *are* salvation. No, we must look to Jesus Himself and His atoning work on the Cross. When by simple heart-trust we appropriate what He did on our behalf in that judicial act of Calvary, we become freed from "condemnation," from the condemnation of the Law (Rom. viii. 1; Gal. iii. 13); that is, we become acquitted, just as though we ourselves had suffered the dread death-penalty of our sins and had thus become discharged by the Law. Moreover, we become "justified" (Rom. v. 1); that is, we become accounted righteous in God's sight; for just as our sin was imputed to Christ when He hung on Calvary as our Sin-bearer, so now His blemishless righteousness is imputed to *us*, and we become covered by it as by a stainless, beautiful robe. And still further, we become "forgiven" by a loving heavenly Father, and restored to the status of "children" to Him (Eph. i. 7; 1 John iii. 1). All this, and much more, is in that wonderful cross of Christ, considered objectively.

But besides all this, salvation through the Christ of Calvary has its subjective and inward and experiential counterpart. As those Israelites, away back in Numbers xxi, not only saw in that objective serpent of brass a symbolic expression of sin that had now been judged, but also felt *within* themselves a new life-flow, healing them of the serpent-virus, so is it with those of us who have looked to Jesus as our Saviour. It is not only that our sin has been judged and that we are now given a new standing before God; something has happened *within* us. We know it. We feel it. We continue to prove it daily. Faith in Christ is no longer a mere experiment; it is an *experience*. It has brought healing for our inward fever, renewal of our inward propensities, and the refining of our hearts by the Holy Spirit. Over against the "law of sin" in our members is the new "law of life" which has become operative within us; so that we can say with Paul, "The law of the Spirit of life in Christ Jesus hath made me free from the law of sin and death" (Rom. viii. 2). The Holy Spirit has deposited a new life within us. He has given us a new nature with heavenly and holy instincts. He has *not* rid us of the very *presence* of sin in and around us, and does not design so to do in this present pilgrimage, any more than He rid the Israelite camp of the hurtful reptiles; but the power of sin is broken, even as the power of the reptiles was broken, for the Cross is ever present, as the brazen serpent was; and from it there continually flows in response to simple faith, a real sense of inward cleansing and healing and renewing, the assurance of a loving heavenly Father's forgiveness, the awareness of a blood-bought peace in the conscience, and the conscious supply of a new energy against temptation. Thus salvation is both objective and subjective, outward and inward; and the more truly we look to "Jesus only," so the more fully do we prove the reality of it.

LIFE FOR A LOOK!

Observe what happens when the cry rises at sea—"A man overboard!" With others on deck you rush to the side, and, leaning over the bulwarks with beating heart, you watch the place where the rising air-bells and boiling deep tell that he has gone down. After some moments of breathless anxiety you see his head emerge from the wave. Now, that man, I shall suppose is no swimmer— he has never learned to breast the billows, yet, with the first breath he draws, he begins to beat the water; with violent effort he attempts to shake off the grasp of death, and by the play of limbs and arms, to keep his head from sinking. It may be that these struggles but exhaust his strength, and sink him all the sooner; nevertheless, that drowning one makes instinctive and convulsive efforts to save himself. So, when first brought to feel and cry, "I perish,"—when the horrible conviction rushes into the soul that we are lost, when we feel ourselves going down beneath a load of guilt into the depth of the wrath of God, our first effort is to save ourselves. Like a drowning man, who will clutch at straws and twigs, we seize on anything, however worthless, that promises salvation. Thus, alas! many poor souls toil and spend weary, unprofitable years in the attempt to establish a righteousness of their own, and find in the deeds of the law protection from its curse.

Thomas Guthrie, D.D.

LIFE FOR A LOOK!

WE HAVE now traced out the main lines of type-teaching in the brazen serpent and its setting; but before we leave this present series of evangelistic interpretations we ought to review the incident *as such*, reading "between the lines," with realistic imagination, and at the same time asking ourselves what the final thought or truth or impression is which it leaves on the mind.

Read the brief story through yet once again. It is wonderful how much is packed into half a dozen verses. And what is the final idea which this typically significant episode leaves with us? It is that of LIFE FOR A LOOK. "Every one that is bitten, when he looketh upon it, shall live." And that is the quite dramatic final parallel with the Gospel of Christ. Amid a scene of sin and death, LIFE FOR A LOOK! Or, to "New Testamentise" it, ETERNAL LIFE SIMPLY BY BELIEVING! That is the vital parallel which our Lord Himself drew, in John iii. 14—"And as Moses lifted up the serpent in the wilderness, even so must the Son of Man be lifted up, that whosoever *believeth in Him* should not perish, but have eternal life."

Get the picture of that vast, serpent-plagued camp of Israel long ago. Let imagination's eye bring it before us again. What a scene of agitation, desperation and woe it was! See that extensive twelve-mile quadrangle, with the large and beautifully coloured Tabernacle in the centre, the tents of Moses, Aaron, and the priests hard by the Tabernacle gate on the east, with the tents of the Merarites, the Gershonites, and the Kohathites in the north and west and south proximity of it; and then, stretching away in every direction from this centre, the tribal suburbs with their lines and lanes of tents, their open clearings for the cattle, their spaces for conference and business exchange, and all the busy activities of that huge, mobile encampment of over two million people.

Literally, there is sobbing and wailing and wringing of hands everywhere. There has never been anything so terrible in memory. There is scarce a family without some casualty. The one dread alarm on everybody's lips is, "The fiery serpents!" Eyes are red with weeping. Cheeks are blanched with fear. No one is safe. The horrible reptiles lurk everywhere. Young and old among the people are attacked without discrimination. Even the most wary are taken by surprise; and to be bitten is certain death. All sorts of expedients have been tried. The people have gone about armed against the fatal pests, but for every serpent killed half a dozen more appear. Lotions and balsams have been applied; herbs have been compounded, and medicines drunk; but all to no avail. People are dying by scores and hundreds, and already "much people of Israel" have died.

There are hurried funerals and interments all round the area of the camp. Over in one direction a mother and her sons stand weeping where a husband and father now lies buried, a serpent-victim. Not far away a young Hebrew and his wife stand in heart-rending grief over a little scar in the desert crust where their young firstborn lies—stung by one of the vipers only the day before, while playing at the tent door. Even as these and other mourners stand at the many different graves, piercing cries and despairing groans fall on their ears from others in the camp who are just newly stung and who know to their terror that within a matter of hours they too will be corpses!

Let imagination transport you to that scene of poignant and helpless sorrow. Stand there amid it all, and then imagine what it must have meant when the news flashed round—"*A cure!*" "*A cure!*" "*A cure!*" Husbands, fathers, mothers, sons, daughters —in their hundreds they dash in and out among those lanes, and with breathless eagerness break into a thousand tents where bitten ones lie dying, and exclaim, "Hurry! A cure! A cure!" And soon, in their hundreds, languishing, fevered, pain-racked, expiring snake-victims are being somehow evacuated from the tents to places where, away beyond the defiles of tents, they can see the shining snake of brass on the high pole! And everywhere there are instantaneous and amazing cures! And everywhere there are exclamations of rapturous joy from the lips of loved ones restored to each other!

Here, in one tent, a mother bends over her dying son. Her heart-strings are torn and bleeding; and she can do nothing but try and soothe him a little in his last moments. But suddenly, in through the awning a neighbour rushes with the news, "A cure! Quick!—your son need not die!" A sentence is enough to explain; and before another moment has expired, loving hands and arms are struggling to get the young fellow where he can see the brazen serpent on the pole. "Look! look! there it is!" cries the mother, as she points away beyond the tents. "Oh, look, look, my son! Can't you see it, shining there?" The young Hebrew has scarcely the strength to lift his head, but he struggles to raise a languid eye to where his mother points. A moment of excruciating suspense! Can he see it? And then, suddenly he says, "Yes, I see it!" And just as suddenly as he sees it, the flush of health spreads over his cheeks; the fever dies away from his throbbing temples; the torpor and stupor vanish from his limbs and faculties; he sits up; he stretches himself in a strange, glad, wide-eyed surprise; he stands, he leaps, he shouts and dances, in a sudden, sheer ecstasy! In a moment, in the twinkling of an eye, he has passed from the pallor of death to the bloom and full vigour of his young manhood again, while his mother looks on in a perfect rapture of astonishment!

Such things, as we can well imagine, would be happening all over that wide-spreading Israelite community; but is it thinkable that anything like the following would take place? Away in one of the tents of the Naphtali allotment, north-east of the Tabernacle, is a young Hebrew fellow who has been stung by one of the fiery vipers as he thrust his hand into the provender gathered for his few beasts; and now he lies waiting for death, with melancholy resignation in his mind, but with growing sensations of the burning poison-fever in his body. It is no use fighting. He has seen many others die of the serpent-venom. He knows that soon the climactic paroxysms will be upon him, and then, soon afterwards, death itself.

But suddenly a neighbour hurries to his side, telling him all about the wonderful cure provided in the uplifted serpent of brass. "Get outside quickly, and look away to the remedy!" urges the neighbour. "Don't delay. I can see you are getting worse every minute. Come! I'll help you." But no, the bitten man is obstinate. "I'm not impressed with that brazen serpent idea," he says. "Others have told me of it, but the more I think about it the more irrational it seems to me. What possible connection can there be between my body and that piece of twisted brass away yonder on that pole? If there had been some special medicine prescribed I would gladly have taken it; or even if the priests had been told to rub that metal serpent into the wound I might have believed then that there was some strange healing property in it; but to think that just a look from here to there can do anything . . .! Clearly the thing is absurd." "Oh, do not be so foolish!" exclaims the neighbour. "The vital thing is not what *you think*, but what *God says*. You haven't got to understand *how* it works before you can prove that it *does* work. Hundreds of others have tried it and proved it. I have seen them almost at the point of death, but they have just been able to raise an eye to the serpent on the pole, and they have been cured on the spot." Even this, however, is not enough for the stubborn victim inside this tent of Naphtali. "Well, well," he gasps, between the now rapidly worsening agues; "it is surprising how credulous some folk are. I'm afraid your words are wasted on me. I could never believe anything which cannot be made acceptable to my reason." And so he dies, with the remedy there but foolishly despised.

Is it thinkable, we ask again, that anything like that would happen in that Israelite camp? Of course not! Once that brass serpent was displayed there, high above the tent tops, people would always see to it that there were clearings made from which anybody could "look" to it without difficulty. Nor would bitten people even linger to wash the wound or bind the limb; they would turn at once, and "look," and be healed. Whenever men know that they are really faced with physical death, they indulge in no procrastination if there is any way of escape. They act at once, with no dallying or arguing. Yet in the matter of *spiritual* death, and the judgment to come, and eternal damnation, which are far more terrible realities than the death of the body, men will argue and pretend and trifle and put off, until they find themselves in the dread, endless soul-death of a Christless eternity!

"If you can explain what possible connection there is between me to-day and the cross of Christ, a thing of two thousand years ago, I might be able to believe," say some. "How could one Person possibly bear the sins of all human beings throughout history?" ask others. But most who so talk or question are only camouflaging. Deep down in their hearts they know the answers to their own questions and objections. The cross of Christ is not merely a thing of two thousand years ago. It is a thing of eternity. What happened on Calvary was but the historical expression of that eternal fact. The cross of Christ was in the heart and counsels of the Godhead before ever Adam was in Eden, even "before the mountains were brought forth." Christ is called "the Lamb slain before the foundation of the world" (Rev. xiii. 8; 1 Pet. i. 20). And as for the problem of *One* bearing the sins of all men, that One is the One who made and sustains the whole universe, even the infinite Son of God!

But why start answering such questions here? Or why start trying to plumb the depthless Divine philosophy of the Atonement? What we need to know first, as hell-deserving sinners perishing in our sins, is not the *philosophy* of the Cross, but the *GOSPEL* of it. Read the word of God again, for the Bible is indeed the word of God, even as Jesus Christ is verily the Son of God. Read that word again. See how great and gracious, how clear and sure, are the invitations and promises and assurances which come to us on the basis of our Lord's atoning death. We could fill pages with precious texts such as John iii. 36: "He that believeth on the Son hath everlasting life"—not merely *may* have; not even *shall* have in the world to come; but "*HATH*" here and now, and with absolute certainty!

Yes, there is "life for a look"! The mystery of the Cross may be too deep for human understanding, but the Gospel *facts* which emerge from it are so simple and clear that the youngest and dullest may grasp them and become saved. Why be like the imaginary case of that obstinate Hebrew who died of "reason" and "philosophy" when he might have been saved by simply "looking," as the hundreds of others were? To those who are like him, we say, "You know your own sin and need and peril, if you will be honest; and you have the sincere testimony of thousands of others who have *proved* the reality of salvation through accepting the Lord Jesus Christ. Why wait until all your questions are answered? Why let supposed intellectual superiority make you the biggest of *fools* in the end, and ruin your soul for eternity? You have enough clear data to act on. Trust God for the rest. Look now to the uplifted standard! There is "life for a look"! Believe now on the Lord Jesus Christ. There is salvation by simply "believing"!

Yes, look by faith to the Lord Jesus on the Cross. Because He did *everything* which was needed to procure your eternal salvation, there is nothing required of you but a contrite-hearted, simple *believing* upon Him. It is as simple as that. Perhaps most of us have heard of the country villager who had learned for the first time that the earth's circumference is about twenty-five thousand miles, and who, when a motor tourist pulled up and asked him how far it was to the next town, replied, "Sir, it is twenty-four thousand nine hundred and ninety-six miles the way you are going; but if you turn round, it's only four!" Those people who proudly or stubbornly refuse salvation through simply believing on the Lord Jesus, preferring their own reasonings and religious efforts, are going the long, long way round which in reality leads them further and further away from true peace with God and the joys of salvation.

I wonder whether in that old-time camp of Israel, even after the brazen serpent had been uplifted, some of those snake-victims resorted to other remedies before they looked to the one which God Himself had provided. Does the thought seem altogether unfeasible? Knowing what human nature is, we cannot quite suppress the suspicion that possibly, even though the bulk of the people had repented, there may have been some who still remained rebellious. We cannot help recalling the fact that besides pedigree Israelites, a "mixed multitude" had come up out of Egypt with the Hebrew tribes, and had exercised a baneful influence among them long enough before ever the brazen serpent incident occurred. Maybe some of these or their offspring, when they saw that the serpent bites *were* being healed at last, would take the defiant attitude that if there *was* thus a cure, then they themselves would find out another one. Some, we may imagine, would try arts of healing learned away back in Egypt. Perhaps some would even resort to magic formulae, for black-art cults existed in that land of ancient wizardry from which this "mixed multitude" had come. Or maybe peculiar ointments would be prepared and herbaceous mixtures concocted. Most likely of all, there would be both external and internal administerings of hyssop (i.e. the caper plant from which even to-day the finest penicillin comes), for those people of old knew well its medicinal virtues.

But if such alternatives *were* foolishly resorted to, what came of them? They simply made suicides. No man-devised substitute, either medical or magical, either external or internal, was of any potency against the deadly blood-poisoning caused by those "fiery serpents." Nor is there any substitute for the cross of Christ. How many unconverted people to-day need to realise this! Salvation comes not by saying the Creed but by seeing the Cross. Salvation is not merely religion, it is redemption. Salvation is not found in a system but in a Saviour. Conversion is not merely turning over a new leaf, it is taking in a new life! It is not simply having a new purpose in life, but being made a new person in Christ. Spiritual healing comes not through psychiatry but through Christopathy!

I wonder if there really *were* people in that old-time Israelite multitude who for *any* reason would not look to the brazen serpent? One can scarcely think it seriously, though some people's minds certainly are capable of strange reactions. Is it thinkable, for instance, that any man among them would haughtily set aside such a way of salvation as foolish and beneath his condescension? If there *were* birds of such fine feather among them, what was the answer to them? Was it to start ratiocinating on the philosophical rationale or the Divine *raison d'être* of that facsimile reptile on the upraised standard? No; the true answer was to point to the scores and hundreds and thousands of living men and women in the camp who had "looked" to the serpent on the pole and had *proved* its healing power in their own bodies. If the elders had reported to Moses that some of the people did not believe in the saving power of the uplifted remedy and were treating it as foolishness, Moses might well have said, "The uplifted serpent of brass is foolishness to them that are perishing in their unbelief, but unto us which are cured by it, it is the power of God unto salvation." Well, if we rightly read the story, Moses had *no need* to talk like that to those people; but centuries later, when the wonderful Gospel of Christ was preached among the peoples of the earth, the apostle Paul *did* need to talk like that. Listen to what he says in 1 Corinthians i. 18, "For the preaching of the Cross is to them that are perishing foolishness; but unto us which are being saved it is the power of God." Do I now address someone who, with pride of learning, scorns the Cross as foolishness? I would say to such an one, "The very fact that you think the Cross to be foolishness is the sure sign that you are a perishing soul, and not at all that you are intellectual." "The preaching of the Cross is to *them that are perishing* foolishness . . ." Proud scorner, think that over carefully!

Whether or not there were people in that long-ago camp of Israel who, for one reason or another, did not look to the uplifted serpent of brass is a point of curiosity beyond the information we possess. We must leave it. But one thing is obvious: as soon as ever Moses erected that serpent of brass on the pole, he created thereby a crisis-point for every snake-bitten Israelite. It was a glad and yet a solemn crisis-point. It was a life and death crisis. There was for every individual a fate-deciding choice to be made. Each one must either "look" and be saved, or refuse and perish. And truly is it so in relation to the cross of Christ. That Cross has created a crisis-point for every son and daughter of Adam. And this becomes accentuatedly so when the Cross is faithfully uplifted before a congregation of people by a preacher of the Gospel. A glad yet infinitely solemn crisis-point is thereby precipitated. Every unsaved sinner is forced to a point of choice. Each one must either accept or reject Christ. To "look" to Him by faith, is to be eternally saved. To close the heart against Him is to confirm oneself in sin and guilt and eternal ruin.

To the sincere Gospel preacher it is at once a subduing and yet an impelling thought that practically every time he preaches the Gospel to a crowd of people he creates the supreme crisis-point for some hearer. It may be that someone whom we now address is confronted again, or perhaps confronted for the first time, with the necessity of making the destiny-involving choice. Earnestly would we urge any such to accept the Lord Jesus as Saviour without delay. And in this connection we would speak the following words of counsel before we close this final address on the brazen serpent.

First; remember that you are to look to the Cross in simple but real faith, not in any superstitious or merely sentimental way. There is much reason for our saying this. Have we not mentioned already that the serpent of brass which Moses erected became superstitiously venerated as time went on, until eventually it became a sort of idol-prophylactic to which incense was burned, and king Hezekiah had to have it destroyed, as recorded in 2 Kings xviii. 4? Alas, for millions of people the same kind of thing has happened even with the cross of Christ. It has been sentimentally reduced or superstitiously perverted into a mere crucifix. But there is all the difference in the world between the true cross of Christ and the Roman Catholic crucifix. It is the former, not the latter, you must look to.

One of the immeasurable evils which the Roman church has inflicted on mankind is that of everywhere displaying Christ as being perpetually pinioned to a cross. Christ is *not* now on the Cross, any more than He is still in the grave. If Christ were still languishing on the Cross, then atonement would not yet be a completed achievement, but only a prolonged and pathetic and uncertain suspense. Even if Christ were now dead but still on the Cross or in the tomb, there would be no Gospel of a completely provided redemption. A dead Christ is no Saviour. Apart from our Lord's resurrection there is no Divine guarantee that the sacrifice on Calvary is accepted of God on man's behalf.

Thank God, everywhere in the pages of the New Testament the Calvary work of our Lord is represented as a *completed* work. Ere He expired on the Cross He exclaimed, "It is finished!" It was not just the sigh of an exhausted sufferer; it was the shout of a conqueror. It proclaimed that His work of atonement on our behalf was now complete. And if it is complete, there is nothing whatever to add to it. Therefore Christ is no longer on the Cross.

Thank God, both the Cross and the tomb are empty! That

empty Cross means sin fully and finally atoned for. That empty sepulchre means Satan vanquished and Christ victorious. There must be no sentimental or superstitious looking to the Christ of the crucifix! When we point men to the Cross, we mean the *real* Cross, that awful yet glorious transaction of substitutionary sin-bearing which happened once for all, never to need repeating, never to need complementing, never to need improving. It is to *that* Cross we point; not to a still-lingering crucifixion and an incompleted offering. As the old hymn says,

> Jesus did it all,
> Long, long ago.

It is to *that* Cross we now point, as the all-sufficient basis on which pardon for sin and peace with God are published to men. It is to *that* Christ we now point, who once died but is now risen and knocking at the door of our hearts. Rest on His Calvary, work for pardon and peace. Open your heart to Jesus Himself, the risen and living One who brings new life and power within! As we have said, faith on Christ for salvation is really very simple; yet there is one point about it which must be made unmistakably clear, namely: Saving faith is not just assenting with the mind; it is *accepting with the heart*.

But further; in looking to Christ be sure that you are really looking to HIM and *away from yourself*. Away back in that snake-swarmed camp of Israel, do you think that when once the brazen serpent was lifted up for their cure, the bitten Israelites spent all their time, or any time at all, examining their wounds to see if they were healing? Were they so silly as to look off from the means of cure to ascertain their progress of recovery? No, they would not have diverted their eye from that brazen serpent even to look at a second sun if it had been kindled at that time in the firmament. They looked *off* from themselves and fixed their gaze on the uplifted remedy; and it was as they looked that their pain assuaged, their fever cooled, and their health returned.

It is very common for persons who are under deep conviction for their sins, and acutely anxious about salvation, to become introspective, to become obsessed with watching their own feelings for signs as to whether they are saved or not. Such solicitude is good, but such *misdirection* of it is bad. Beware against this misdirected solicitude. If you *do* look within yourself, let it only be to know how truly you need salvation, not to try and find any consolation. Look away from yourself, and away from all your wounds, to the uplifted Saviour. *His* wounds will heal yours. *His* death is your life. *His* Cross is your cure. As you look to HIM you are saved, quite apart from what you may feel within yourself.

But perhaps this only causes some anxious seeker to ask, "*Ought* I not to *feel* within myself that I am saved, even though I do look away from myself to Christ? Did not those snake-bitten Israelites feel in their own bodies that they were cured when they looked off to the brazen serpent?" Well, it is a fact, of course, that when the body is ill we know it, sooner or later, because we *feel* it. But when the body is *well* we do not know *that* because we have a continuous succession of nervous thrills! Health is often at its best when least conscious of itself. When those Israelites of old were cured, the transition was not one from pain and weakness to a state of *strange sensations*! Nor must those who are seeking salvation in Jesus Christ mistakenly suppose that the evidences of it are necessarily emotional disturbances. Mind you, if there is a really sincere repentance toward God, and a real burden on the mind because of sin, and then a real resting of the heart upon Jesus for salvation, it is almost a certainty that there will be a conscious sense of relief, a sense of new-found peace with God. All genuine conversions to Christ are followed by the inward witness of God's Holy Spirit; but the point is that we are not to look *only for that* when we come to Christ for salvation. The *fact* of salvation is more important than the *feeling* of it.

When we have accepted Christ as our Saviour, there are three ways by which we may know that we are saved. First, we have the guarantee of it in black and white, in the inspired word of God: "These things have I written unto you that believe on the name of the Son of God, THAT YE MAY KNOW that ye have ETERNAL LIFE" (1 John v. 13). Second, we have the evidence

of it in *changed desires*, even though these changed desires are
not accompanied by emotional ecstacies. We now hate the sins
which once we loved. The spell of the world is broken, and we
lose our appetite for its hollow, unspiritual and godless pleasures.
We now have desires toward God and spiritual things; and we
love those very things which once had no attraction for us. Why,
this change of desires is enough in itself of *inward* evidence to
prove to us that a saving work has happened in the heart. But
third, and in addition to this, if besides accepting Christ as
Saviour we really yield ourselves fully to Him, it is not long
before we become aware that God's own Holy Spirit is inwardly
witnessing to our hearts that we are the regenerated children
of God. As 1 John v. 10 says, "He that believeth on the Son
hath the witness in himself." And as Romans viii. 16 says, "The
Spirit Himself beareth witness with our spirits that we are the
children of God."

Yes, it certainly is true that those Israelites of old knew in
themselves that they had been healed; and it is similarly true
that Christian believers know in themselves that they have been
saved; but that is not the *first* thing for *seekers* after salvation
to be concerning themselves about. Look to Jesus alone, apart
from all inward feelings. Believe His word of promise in the
Gospel—"that whosoever *believeth* on HIM should not perish,
but have eternal life." As old Dr. F. B. Meyer used to say, the
true order is FACT . . . FAITH . . . FEELING. Get right
on the *fact* first, that Jesus really took your place and bore your
sin on Calvary. Then really exercise *faith* toward that fact. And
the inward *feeling* will come sooner or later, either suddenly or
gradually.

Does someone say, "I want to believe upon Jesus, but I *cannot*; I cannot unless God's Spirit moves me and gives me the
faith to believe"? You are wrong. Satan deceives you. You are
a free agent. You *can* accept Jesus this moment if you will.
Deep down in your heart you know it. In Revelation x. 3, we
read that "seven thunders uttered their voices." Even so, in the
heart of man there are seven thunders which continually utter
the freedom and responsibility of the human will—"I am," "I
think," "I reason," "I love," "I judge," "I choose," "I act."

And the very last appeal in the Bible is an appeal to the will
—"Whosoever *will* . . ." Yes, you can if you will. Oh, that
you *may*!

Does someone else say, "I want to believe on Jesus, but I am
sure that my condition is too bad at present. I must somehow
try to improve myself first"? Such a way of reasoning is a tangle
of contradiction. It is even less sensible than saying, "I really
am critically ill; I am too ill for the doctor at present; but I
will make myself better a bit, and then send round for him."
The bigger sinners we are, the greater is our need to come to
Jesus for salvation at once, and the bigger reason we have for
coming, and the bigger glory it is to the grace of God for saving us!

> Let not conscience make you linger,
>   Nor of fitness fondly dream;
> All the fitness He requireth
>   Is your heartfelt need of Him.

> Come ye weary, heavy-laden,
>   Bruised and ruined by the Fall;
> If you tarry till you're better,
>   You will never come at all.

A father received word that his son, a brilliant lad, had been
killed in the war. Turning to his minister, he cried in desperation, "Tell me, sir, where was God when my boy was killed?"
In that tense moment guidance was given to the minister. "My
friend," he said, "God was just where He was when His own Son
was killed." God was *at* the Cross, and *in* His Son, when the
Saviour hung on Calvary. As Paul says, "God was in Christ
reconciling the world unto Himself." God is still there. That
is where He still meets repenting sinners. He waits there now.
He waits to be gracious. Where sin abounds, grace much more
abounds. The Cross is still "the power of God unto salvation,
to everyone that believeth." "He that believeth on the Son
hath everlasting life." Yes, it is true—"*There is life for a look*"!
"As Moses lifted up the serpent in the wilderness, even so must
the Son of Man be lifted up; that whosoever believeth in Him

should not perish, but have eternal life. FOR GOD SO LOVED THE WORLD THAT HE GAVE HIS ONLY BEGOTTEN SON, THAT WHOSOEVER BELIEVETH IN HIM SHOULD NOT PERISH, BUT HAVE EVERLASTING LIFE."

There is life for a look at the crucified One,
    There is life at this moment for thee;
Then look, sinner, look unto Him and be saved,
    Unto Him who was nailed to the tree.

It is not thy tears of repentance or prayers,
    But the *blood* that atones for the soul;
On Him, then, who shed it thou mayest at once
    Thy weight of iniquity roll.

Then take with rejoicing from Jesus at once
    The life everlasting He gives;
And know with assurance thou never canst die,
    Since Jesus, thy righteousness, lives.